YOU CAN HAVE IT ALL

YOU CAN HAVE IT ALL

UNLOCK THE SECRETS TO A GREAT LIFE

GAUR GOPAL DAS

THE VOICE OF WISDOM FOR THE
MODERN WORLD

HARPER
NON-FICTION

First published in India by Harper Non-Fiction 2026
An imprint of HarperCollins *Publishers*
HarperCollins *Publishers* India, Cyber City, Building 10-A,
Gurugram, Haryana-122002, India
www.harpercollins.co.in

2 4 6 8 10 9 7 5 3 1

Text copyright © Gaur Gopal Das 2026
Illustrations copyright © Veer Misra 2026

P-ISBN: 978-93-6989-132-0
E-ISBN: 978-93-6989-660-8

All characters and incidents described in this book are the product of the author's imagination. Any resemblance to actual persons, living or dead, is entirely coincidental.

The views and opinions expressed in this book are the author's own and the facts are as reported by him, and the publishers are not in any way liable for the same.

Gaur Gopal Das asserts the moral right
to be identified as the author of this work.

All rights reserved. No part of this publication may be reproduced, stored in a retrieval system, or transmitted, in any form or by any means, electronic, mechanical, photocopying, recording or otherwise, without the prior permission of the publishers.

Without limiting the exclusive rights of any author, contributor or the publisher of this publication, any unauthorized use of this publication to train generative artificial intelligence (AI) technologies is expressly prohibited. HarperCollins also exercise their rights under Article 4(3) of the Digital Single Market Directive 2019/790 and expressly reserve this publication from the text and data-mining exception.

Typeset in 11.5/15.7 Adobe Caslon Pro
by HarperCollins *Publishers* India Pvt. Ltd

Printed and bound at
Replika Press Pvt. Ltd.

This book is produced from independently certified FSC® paper
to ensure responsible forest management.
*

HarperCollins Publishers, Macken House, 39/40 Mayor Street Upper,
Dublin 1, D01 C9W8, Ireland

*To my beloved Spiritual Master,
His Holiness Radhanath Swami Maharaj,
whose wisdom and compassion continue
to illuminate countless lives—
offered with love on his seventy-fifth birthday*

The detailed notes pertaining to this book are available on the HarperCollins *Publishers* India website. Scan this QR code to access the same.

Contents

Author's Note ... ix

1. **HASHTAGS, HOODIES AND A MONK** ... 1
   Discovering the Three Dimensions of Understanding Relationships

2. **THE GAME OF SNAKES AND LADDERS** ... 27
   Navigating Failure and Finding True Success

3. **CRACKED MUGS** ... 54
   Finding Beauty and Acceptance in Imperfection

4. **THE WISDOM OF THE LOTUS** ... 76
   How to Move from Lack to Fulfilment

5. **THE MEHENDI MOSAIC** ... 104
   Giving Colour to Unspoken Dreams

6. **STANDING STILL WITHIN A STORM** ... 126
   Building Your Foundations of Inner Strength

7. **THE ONE-HANDED MONK** ... 147
   The Life-Changing Magic of Real Communication

8. **SACRED HALDI** — 171
   The Power of Vulnerability

9. **UNFINISHED STORIES** — 197
   Finding Clarity without Closure

10. **A WELL-BAKED CAKE** — 217
    Aligning Thought and Action

11. **A MONK AT THE MANDAP** — 242
    Can We Have It All?

Your Thought Journal — 254

Notes — 292

Author's Note

=

First and foremost, dear reader, I want to express my heartfelt gratitude for the incredible love you've shown towards my first two books and all the content I share—whether on social media or through Monkify, the little app we built to help you strengthen your inner foundation. You've been a part of this journey, and I'm deeply grateful.

This book brings together ten life-changing principles woven into an engaging story with characters you might just see a bit of yourself in. Each chapter is inspired by real stories, emotions and experiences. Though many details have been reshaped to maintain the rhythm of this narrative—and most names and places changed to honour privacy—the essence, the truth, remains untouched.

Feel free to simply enjoy the stories and the wisdom they carry. Or if you'd like to make the experience more personal and practical, you'll find worksheets designed to help you reflect on and apply these principles in your own life. To keep the reading experience smooth, these worksheets have been included at the end of the book for those who prefer pen and paper. And for readers who enjoy the digital format, a QR code (on page 254) will lead you to Monkify, where you can fill them in online.

This book is meant to guide, inspire and support you on your journey of inner growth and self-discovery. It is not a substitute for professional medical, psychological or therapeutic advice, diagnosis or treatment. If you ever feel overwhelmed or are struggling emotionally or physically, please reach out to a qualified professional, a trusted friend or a counsellor. Seeking help is not a sign of weakness—it's a sign of wisdom and self-care.

The reflections, exercises and stories in these pages are shared with love and sincerity—meant to complement your journey, not replace your own judgement or professional guidance. Take away what resonates, pause where you need to and allow the process to unfold gently.

My sincerest gratitude to my gurus, teachers, family, friends, team members and every well-wisher who has supported me—silently or visibly—along the way.

A heartfelt thank you to HarperCollins India and their wonderful team for believing in this vision and bringing it to life. Special thanks to my editor, Ms Trisha Bora, and Ms Poulomi Chatterjee, Ms Rachita Raj and Ms Gayatri Goswami in the editorial team. Thank you, Mr Saurav Das and Mr Veer Misra, for your designs and illustrations, and Mr Rajan Yadav for your typesetting.

And finally, to you, dear reader—for choosing to spend your time on these pages. I truly hope that, by God's grace, this book helps you unlock the secrets to having it all—peace, purpose and joy—right where you are.

1

Hashtags, Hoodies and a Monk

Discovering the Three Dimensions of Understanding Relationships

∼

Life asks us three questions again and again: Do you understand others? Do you understand yourself? And do you understand why you are here?

Our answers to these questions shape everything else.

It was the sort of wedding that came with its own hashtag, logo, drone coverage and five wedding planners—two for the bride, two for the groom and one on standby in case the first four had creative differences.

The invitation was no less than a movie poster:

> *Rohan & Sanjana invite you to their Grand Royal Wedding Weekend at the heritage Haveli Palace, Jaisalmer, Rajasthan*
> *#SanjRohShaadi #PalacePromiseForever*

And under 'Dress Code', it proudly declared:
- Arrival Evening: *Terrace Soirée*
- Day 1: *Mehendi Royal*
- Day 1.5: *Bollywood Bling*
- Day 2: *Desert Chic*
- Day 2.5: *Sunset Gold*
- Day 3: *Regal Radiance*
- Departure Morning: *Recovery Casual*

When a wedding schedule has more decimal points than a math textbook, you know it's going to be intense!

This was my friend Rakesh Arora's son Rohan's wedding. Rakesh and I had known each other for a little over two years, and in that short time we'd become close friends. With him being a dear friend—and me being a monk—it wasn't really a surprise that he invited me. In fact, in India, not inviting a monk to a wedding is considered more inauspicious than forgetting the groom's sehra.

Now, I barely understood what 'Desert Chic' or 'Sunset Gold' or any of the other dress codes were supposed to mean. But 'Recovery Casual'? That one I fully supported. After three days of nonstop festivities, glitter, endless selfies and buffet plates heavier than dumbbells, who wouldn't need half a day for recovery?

Luckily, my wardrobe posed no such problems. My dress code is permanently fixed: one style, every day. Orange robes. Bald head (by choice—I haven't lost my hair; I voluntarily gave it up). Clean-shaven face. That's it. No decision fatigue. No standing in front of a mirror wondering: Beard or moustache today? Side fade or man bun? Desert chic or deserted chic?

I once even joked that having a bald head was such an advantage, I didn't have to waste time grooming my hair. Someone immediately replied, 'True, but there's a disadvantage—you don't know where to stop washing your face. There's no boundary!'

So I landed at Jaisalmer airport—a tiny desert outpost that looks less like an airport and more like a bus stop with aspirations. One baggage belt, one exit gate and about seven camels loitering outside like unofficial greeters.

From here, it was a forty-minute drive to the Haveli Palace, the venue of the hashtag-heavy #SanjRohShaadi. A palace full of sparkle, gold and family drama ... and me, a monk with a strolley small enough to fit inside the glove compartment of a car.

As I stepped out of the arrival gate, the air was warm and dry. The November desert heat was softened by a mild breeze, but it was still hot enough to make you question any clothing choice beyond cotton wear.

And there he was. A slim teenager, barely nineteen, holding a small 'Welcome' placard that was half hidden behind his phone. He had the unmistakable Gen Z look—oversized hoodie in the desert heat (fashion, not logic), sneakers that probably cost more than his entire college tuition fees and wireless earbuds hanging like a tech-inspired necklace. His hair was carefully styled to look carelessly messy, with faint silver-blonde highlights at the tips—a lot of effort spent to look effortless. Slung over his shoulder was a canvas tote, its corner weighed down by a sketchbook peeking out—the edges curled, the paper smudged with graphite—as though it had travelled with him more through stories than pages.

This was Ved, grandson of my friend Rakesh. We had never met before.

Ved glanced up from his phone, spotted me in my saffron robes and paused for a second. Then he offered a polite half-smile—the kind teenagers give when they're not sure if they should be respectful, friendly or simply refrain from conveying the irony of a situation.

'Hi ... umm ... Gaur Gopal Das? I'm Ved. My grandfather sent me to receive you,' he said, slightly awkward but sincere.

I nodded warmly. 'Thank you, Ved. Nice to meet you.'

He gave a quick nod in return and gestured towards the waiting area. 'Shall we?'

We walked to where a sleek black Mercedes-Benz S-Class stood with its engine humming, a uniformed chauffeur waiting to take our bags. We slid into the car.

I was touched that Rakesh had sent a family member to receive me rather than simply sending a nice pick-up car. I travel a lot for work these days, and when I arrive at these events, people want to shower me with their gratitude. So naturally, I get picked up in luxury sedans that cost more than the lifetime value of my bank account. I'm given five-star-hotel suites so big that I sometimes get lost trying to find the bathroom. And waiting on the table? A welcome platter with fourteen kinds of exotic fruits—thirteen of which I can't even pronounce the name of, let alone eat.

I often joke, 'What most people work their entire lives to procure, I receive as a passing gift. Choose your career wisely!'

But let me be clear—that's just a joke (before anyone here starts enrolling in monk school for the perks).

Because real monk life is quite the opposite. My 'personal residence' is an 8-by-8-feet room in our Mumbai ashram. There's no personal chef drawing up bespoke menus—just a community kitchen serving over eighty monks from every corner of India. You can well imagine the predicament of the poor cooks who try to please everyone. On days when sambar and rice are served, our Punjabi brothers look at the plate as if it's loaded with hospital food. And when it's chole-bhature day, the monks from southern India look like they've just been punished.

That's ashram life—simple, democratic and never boring.

And yet, one of the deepest lessons I've learned on this path is how to gracefully accept love in whatever form it comes. Sometimes it's a luxury car, sometimes it's a simple meal on the floor of someone's modest home. What matters is not the gesture but the feeling behind it.

Sometimes the gesture is small but the feeling behind it is huge. And at times the gesture is big, but the feeling behind it is missing. Which one would you rather receive? If a child offers you half a biscuit with sticky fingers, the gesture carries more heart than someone handing you an expensive pen with zero emotion. One is a gift of the hand. The other is a gift of the heart. And only one truly nourishes us. It's not that material things are bad, but if they aren't backed by feeling they lose their meaning.

The Bhakti tradition that I follow taught me early: Don't just see the object—feel the intention. Don't just count the gesture—cherish the love.

Epic stories like the Mahabharata illustrate this very well. When Shri Krishna visited Hastinapura with his peace proposal, Duryodhana tried to bribe him over to his side with lavish hospitality—a grand palace to stay in, fine clothes and ornaments and a royal feast of fifty-six preparations, delicacies meant to impress. But Shri Krishna declined, saying, 'One accepts an offering for two reasons—either out of hunger, or because it is given with love. I am neither hungry, nor is this offered with love.'

Instead, he went to the humble abode of his devotee Vidura. Vidura was not at home, and his wife, overwhelmed with devotion at Shri Krishna's arrival, rushed to serve him. She offered him a very simple meal. Some folk versions say that in her ecstasy, she peeled bananas—but in her distraction, she mistakenly offered him the peels instead of the fruit. Yet Shri Krishna, smiling, ate them with delight. Why? Because He was tasting the love, not the object.

The lesson is timeless. The world counts the number of dishes, the size of the gift, the price of the jewel—the form. But those who value substance look beyond the form—they measure the heart.

As the Bhagavad Gita says:
*patraṁ puṣpaṁ phalaṁ toyaṁ
yo me bhaktyā prayacchati
tad ahaṁ bhakty-upahṛtam
aśnāmi prayatātmanaḥ*

*Whatever is offered with love and devotion,
Be it a leaf, a flower, a fruit or water,
I graciously accept it.* (9.26)

Things will fade, but feelings remain. Cars get old, hotel suites get checked out of, fruits get eaten ... But the love we felt when these were offered? That stays.

∽

Ved leaned back in his seat, scrolling casually on his phone. The chauffeur adjusted the mirror; the desert road stretched out in front of us. A few minutes into the drive, Ved put down his phone and turned to me. 'So ... what does your name actually mean? Gaur Gopal Das ... it's kinda long.'

I smiled. 'Ah, at least you said it right. Most people get creative with it. Once, someone introduced me as "Gold Gopal Das". I told him, "Sure ... but at what price for 10 grams?"'

Ved slapped his forehead with a grin. 'Gold! Oh man, that's brilliant.'

'And another time,' I continued, 'an airport staff member called me "Mr Gol Gopal Das". Look, I know I have a round face, highlighted even more by my shaved head ... but I'm not exactly gol-matol!'

Ved let out a roar of amusement. 'Gol-matol? That's hilarious!'

'And once at a corporate event, they printed my name as "Gaurav Global Das". For a moment I felt less like a monk and more like a multinational company.'

Ved clapped his hands in delight. 'That one's my favourite. Gaurav Global Das—CEO monk.'

We both broke into laughter.

Then I said more gently, 'But my name was actually given to me by my spiritual teacher—my guru—when I joined the ashram. All of us disciples are given names during our initiation. Men have the suffix *das*, women *dasi*.'

Ved gave me a questioning look. 'Why always das or dasi?'

'Because das means "servant". My guru once told me, "Of everything in your name, the most important part is das. Always remember—you are a servant of God and a servant of others."'

Ved frowned. 'But ... servant? Doesn't that sound kinda insulting? Like ... lowly?'

'That's because the word has been misused. When it first appeared in older texts, the word "servant" carried dignity—someone who served out of loyalty, devotion or duty. For instance, in Trivandrum, Kerala, the royal family formally declared themselves Shri Padmanabha Dasa and Shri Padmanabha Sevini—titles meaning "the servant of Lord Padmanabha", the presiding deity of the kingdom. Male members used the term Dasa and female members Sevini, acknowledging that they ruled not as masters but as servants of God. Even today, the family continues to use these titles.[1] Similarly, in the Bhakti tradition, saints and devotees took names like Tulsidas or Surdas as a mark of humility and love.

'And this wasn't unique to India. In medieval Europe, nobles and statesmen used the same sentiment. Figures like Sir Thomas More would often sign letters with "your humble servant"—not as a put-down, but as a sign of deep respect and loyalty.

'Over time, however, the word transformed. In the age of colonialism and slavery, "servant" began to be equated with bondage and inferiority. Yet there's a world of difference between the two. Slavery is forced. Servitude is a choice.'

Ved raised an eyebrow. 'A choice?'

'Yes. Think about it. Isn't the sign of love to serve the one we love? A mother serves her child without hesitation. Friends serve each other in times of need. Lovers serve each other in small, caring ways. None of that is degrading. It's love in action.'

Ved leaned back. 'Hmm. So you're saying being a servant isn't about low status, and that serving can come from love?'

'Exactly. And imagine if in our relationships we stopped playing the boss and instead tried to serve. Not one-sided service, but both sides, with that spirit. What a beautiful, harmonious relationship that would be.'

'So your name basically says …' he said, his lips curving into a respectful smile, 'you're the servant guy?'

I chuckled. 'Yes. Though I've also been introduced as "Gopal Boss". That's when I had to correct them—the whole point is, I'm not the boss. And even when life places us in the role of a boss or leader, true leadership is about service—serving those whom we are meant to guide.'

Ved shook his head playfully. 'All right, servant guy ... just joking. I think I'm going to call you Gaurji, if that's okay?'

I grinned. 'Of course. Whatever works for you. It's not the label, it's the love behind it that counts.'

There was a moment's silence as Ved returned to his phone. A minute later, a grin spread across his face. 'Wait ... You've got, like, millions of followers on social media? You're basically a celebrity monk!'

I raised an eyebrow. 'Celebrity monk? That sounds like an oxymoron.' I added more softly, 'But really, Ved ... people and their love make me who I am. Who would I be if no one watched the content or cared for what I shared? They're the celebrity. I'm just the servant—the das—and I'm trying my best to be a sincere one.'

Ved's expression softened. 'That's ... actually pretty cool.'

Here we were, two people from two entirely different worlds. A Gen Z teenager who probably communicates more in emojis and acronyms than in full sentences and a monk who sometimes still thinks 'DM' means 'district magistrate'. This ride, I realized, wasn't just going to be a drive to the palace. It was going to be two very different worlds coming together—saffron and sneakers, prayers and playlists. This boy was a living example of the generation gap that had been on my mind these days. And while I hadn't expected it, my conversation with Ved was already peeling back the many layers of what it truly means to understand people from different generations and backgrounds.

∽

Whether in families, workplaces or even among monks, one of the biggest challenges we face today is the generation gap. Never before has there been such a dramatic difference in lifestyles, mindsets, beliefs and expectations—all within the same family.

One generation saves money in fixed deposits, the next puts it into crypto. One is used to carefully writing long letters, the next types 'k' or sends a thumbs-up emoji to acknowledge just about everything. One finds pride in stability, the other values flexibility.

Neither is right or wrong—it's just a different lens they both look through.

I often explain it this way: Two people can look at the same number, one from this side, the other from that side. One insists it's a 6. The other swears it's a 9. And both are right—from where they stand.

But what if, just once, we walked around and looked from the other side? To see what the other person sees? Even if we don't agree, at least we'll understand. And sometimes understanding is more important than being in agreement. Because beneath all the differences—crypto vs fixed deposits, emojis vs letters, hoodies vs robes—lies the same human need. The need to be understood, to be respected, to be loved.

This reminds me of the story of a teacher who held up a mango and asked the class to describe it.

One student said, 'It's yellow.' Another said, 'It's green.' A third said, 'No, no, it's red.' Soon, they were all arguing.

The teacher smiled and said, 'You're all correct. From where you're sitting, you see a different side of the fruit. Only when you walk around it will you see the whole picture.'

Life is like that mango. Relationships, generation gaps, even workplace conflicts—they're not about proving who's right or wrong. They're about whether or not we're willing to walk a few extra steps to see the other side.

And I think that each of us, dear friends, comes to the realization in our own way. This was how I learned to view the whole mango.

When I joined the ashram, I carried with me the small-town upbringing of a boy from a conservative family. Back home, using slang was uncommon—almost unheard of. In fact, I hadn't used any until I moved into the monastery. Our ashram was in downtown Mumbai, and most of the monks were raised in the city as well. Some had studied and even worked in the city before moving in.

Those first few days were a culture shock for me. Here were austere, sincere, deeply devoted monks who, in casual conversation, would use language that rattled me. If someone passed away, they'd say, '*Off ho gaya.*' If someone was being irritating, they'd joke, '*Dimaag ka dahi mat kar* [Don't scramble my brain]!' It amused me, but it also put me off. How could such serious men of God speak like this?

And then, one day, to their shock—and mine—I caught myself saying, '*Lafda ho gaya* [There's a mess-up].' We all burst out laughing.

That moment taught me something important. Sometimes, without even realizing it, we absorb the habits, language and ways of those around us. And so, I resolved to be careful and conscious about what I was absorbing.

Not long after, during a lecture, I heard a senior monk say: 'Don't just see the *what*. Go beyond the *what*. See the *why*.'

The idea struck me deeply. I knew *what* these monks were doing—using slang. But *why*? Because they had grown up in Mumbai. These were the nuances of their everyday language. And yet, despite that, here they were in the ashram, earnestly refining themselves, struggling to improve, offering their lives in service. Their words sometimes carried the flavour of their backgrounds, but their sincerity was pure gold. That day, I learned to see from their point of view. I began looking for the why behind the what. I moved from only seeing a 6 to trying to see how they were seeing a 9.

When there is effort from both sides, relationships become better because we can be empathetic about people's actions, words and motivations before jumping to conclusions. This leads to a deeper sense of understanding and trust.

A couple of months later, I learned the same lesson again—this time in a different manner.

There was a monk who had begun interfering with a role I'd been given at the ashram. Without a word, he had started doing one of the things that had been assigned to me. I felt intruded upon. There was no conversation, no explanation—just intrusion.

I went to a senior monk and opened up about what was bothering me. He listened and said, 'Apart from this one service, you have four others that you can do well. But he has only this one. For you, it is one among many. For him, it is everything. He may be going about it in the wrong way, but why he is doing it is clear—it's his unaddressed need that is surfacing in his behaviour.'

The senior monk assured me he would engage the monk in a way that fulfilled his need, while also helping him see my viewpoint. And in that moment, I understood something deeper: The 6–9 principle isn't just about different generations or backgrounds, it's also about different needs.

In your life, too, you will have such moments. Perhaps you already do. Misunderstandings arise, conflicts surface, issues appear. And that's okay. None of us is perfect. We're all striving to be better.

The real question is: What steps can you and the other person take to better understand each other's needs, concerns and perspectives?

Understanding each other is not only the foundation of strong relationships, it is also the basis of harmonious living in our everyday dealings.

However, there is another layer, the most important one.

Understanding others creates harmony, yes—but in order to begin that journey we must first understand ourselves. That lays the foundation for our relationship with our own inner being. Our relationships with others are only as deep and effective as our relationship with ourselves. When we understand ourselves, when we address our own needs first, only then from that fulfilled state are we better able to understand and address the needs of others.

~

We sat in silence for a while, Ved looking out of the window at the shimmering desert outside. But it didn't hold his attention for long. Soon, he turned to me with a smile.

'So … Gaurji,' Ved said, continuing our conversation, 'what about my name, then? My nani keeps saying Ved means wisdom or knowledge or something?'

I nodded. 'Yes. In Sanskrit, Ved comes from "vid", meaning "to know", "to understand". Not just to collect information, but to have deep wisdom. See, today, we know so much about the world—celebrity scandals, meme trends, the net worth of billionaires …'

'Don't forget digital scams, online conspiracies and Insta breakups.'

I laughed. 'Exactly! We're flooded with information, but very few people actually know who they are. But that's where wisdom begins. Wisdom is knowing yourself—your needs, your triggers, your peace, your happiness.'

'Okay,' he said, leaning forward, 'but how does someone know what they need? Like you said, understand yourself. That sounds nice … But how?'

I smiled. 'Good question. Let me share something from my own journey. You know, there was a time when I was doing so much outreach—sharing messages, guiding others, trying to make a difference—that I got extremely busy.'

Ved raised an eyebrow. 'Being busy helping people sounds like a good problem to have.'

'It is.' I nodded. 'And honestly, the appreciation I got, and seeing lives change, became my fuel to keep doing more.'

'So ... what's the problem? Sounds like a win-win.'

'That's what I thought too,' I said. 'But once, during a particularly busy stretch, I lost my voice—literally. After weeks of travelling and speaking, my throat finally gave up. The doctor ordered complete silence for a few days. At first, I was restless. I wanted to communicate, to keep doing things. But silence has a way of teaching you what noise can't. When you can't speak, you start listening differently—to others, to life, even to yourself.

'In that quiet, I realized how often we move through life responding to expectations, routines or roles without pausing to ask, "What do *I* really need right now?" Those few days of silence taught me a crucial lesson: We often discover our real needs not in the noise of doing, but in the stillness of listening. Sometimes, the universe reminds us of this gently, sometimes strongly—through people, through circumstances or through a jolt that makes us pause. For me, it was my lost voice.'

Ved leaned back thoughtfully. 'So basically, I should lose my voice once in a while?'

'No need to lose your voice,' I joked. 'Just your phone battery will do—the silence that ensues after the phone is drained of charge can be very enlightening.'

Then, returning to the question he'd asked, I said, 'You were asking how we can know what our needs are—that's how. We need to slow down a little and learn to listen to our inner voice. Because if we don't, life finds its own ways to get our attention. But why wait for something painful when we can consciously understand and address our needs?'

Ved tilted his head with a half-smile. 'So ... the universe gives signs, silence gives answers and my generation gives ... notifications. But even monks have their own challenges—that's kinda comforting.'

I laughed. 'Yes, Ved. Even monks. We're all works in progress. The truth is we learn, we slip, we reflect and we realign. That's how growth really works.'

Ved sat up straighter, clearly interested now. 'But what did you actually do to reconnect with yourself?'

'If you truly want to know, I can explain. But it will take some of your time ... and a little patience. Basically, some gyan time.'

Ved grinned. 'Gyan time, huh? All right, I'm game.'

I chuckled. 'Deal. One bite-sized TED Talk coming right up. So here's my model: Pause. Reflect. Experiment.'

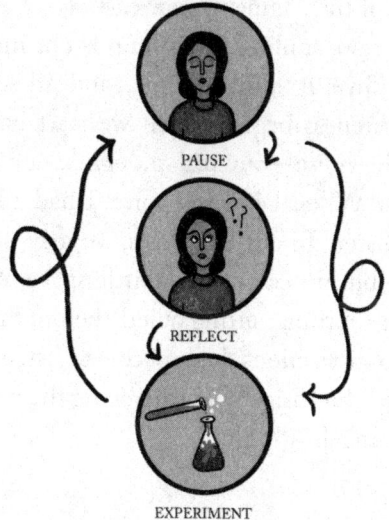

'Okay … sounds simple enough. But what does that even mean?'

'First, *pause*,' I said. 'Life won't pause for you—you have to pause for yourself.'

Ved frowned slightly. 'Pause? Like … meditate?'

'Not necessarily,' I said. 'Pausing doesn't always mean sitting cross-legged or closing your eyes. It simply means stopping the rush long enough to notice what's really happening inside you. To step out of the current, even for a moment, and see where it's carrying you.'

I leaned back, choosing my words carefully. 'At first, it feels uncomfortable, almost unnatural. The mind starts fidgeting. You remember things you forgot to do. You reach for your phone. You realize how noisy your head is. That's normal. We're used to movement; stillness feels strange.'

Ved nodded slowly. 'So it's like … when you turn off the engine after a long drive, and the car is silent, but you still hear the hum of the engine in your ears?'

'Exactly,' I said, smiling. 'That hum is our mind's leftover momentum. Give it a little time, and it settles. That's when real awareness begins, when we start hearing what's underneath the noise—our real thoughts, our real feelings, our real needs. When I lost my voice, I had all the time in the world to listen. In our busy lives, we may not be around such silence—but we can create a little space for it. Just ten minutes in the morning, sitting quietly before the day begins. No phone. No distractions. Just space—to listen.'

Ved nodded. 'So basically … stop being the main character in a never-ending-hustle reel?'

I chuckled. 'Yes. Step away from reel life and into real life.

'Second, *reflect*,' I continued. 'Reflection is the bridge between busyness and balance. During that pause—whether in the morning, evening or whenever we find a little time in the day—we can ask ourselves three questions: What am I feeling? Why am I feeling it? What do I really need right now? I began asking myself these questions often during the time I was resting my voice, and the answers were rarely the same. Some days, I needed patience. Other days, rest. And sometimes, just a little joy.'

Ved squinted. 'You actually answered those questions? Like, for real?'

'Yes,' I said. 'At first, the answers were vague. They came to me in simple terms, such as: "I'm tired" or "I feel restless." But if you persist with this exercise, your inner voice will grow clearer and stronger. And when you honour that voice, you begin to align your actions with your deeper needs. Your inner voice can help you listen to your needs instead of running on autopilot.

'And finally, *experiment*. Reflection without action is just thought. Take small steps to meet the needs you uncover. Treat life like a living laboratory—try, learn, adjust. Over time, these small experiments become habits, and those habits become transformation. Once we know what we need, we can start weaving it into our day. If we need rest, we sleep a little earlier. If we need focus, we cut out distractions. And if we need joy, we make the time to laugh with someone.'

Ved grinned. 'Okay, so ... your big monk secret is trial and error?'

I laughed. 'Yes. Trial, error, learn, repeat. That's how growth works. Pause. Reflect. Experiment. And the best part—you can start practising right now. Self-knowledge is less like a Google search and more like a lab experiment—you discover it bit by bit.'

'Hmm ... I can't just download the Know Yourself app?' Ved chuckled.

'Nope.' I replied. 'The app is already installed inside you. You just need to open it more often than you open Instagram to see your crush's story.'

Ved shook his head and quickly glanced back at his phone—the way teenagers often do when humour brushes close to something personal.

What I think Ved was discovering in our conversation is something we all struggle with too, isn't it?

We're all always running around—catering to the demands of family, work and social circles. We're so connected to the world that somewhere along the way, we forget ourselves. The Urdu poet Bashar captured this predicament perfectly:

> *Unhe kamyabi mein sukoon nazar aaya toh woh daudte gaye,*
> *Humein sukoon mein kamyabi dikhi toh hum thehar gaye!*
> *Khwahisho ke bojh mein, Bashar ... tu kya kya kar raha hai ...*
> *Itna toh jeena bhi nahi jitna tu mar raha hai ...*

> *They saw peace in success and so they kept running,*
> *We saw success in peace, and so we paused!*
> *Under the burden of desires, O Bashar, what all are you chasing ...*
> *You are dying far more than you are living ...*

Yes, there will always be demands and responsibilities, deadlines to meet, desires to fulfil and dreams to chase. But if we do it all at the cost of our own peace, we lose the very essence of why we are striving in the first place. This is the art of truly understanding yourself:

Pause to make space.
Reflect to listen within.
Experiment to grow in alignment with what you find.

By doing these practices regularly—even for a few minutes a day—we begin to tone the muscle of self-awareness. Over time, these small pauses and reflections add up. They help us understand our needs, desires, motivations and, ultimately, who we really are.

I noticed Ved still half-distracted by his screen, so I decided to pull him back. I leaned in with a grin.

'And here's the twist,' I said. 'In Marathi, "Ved"—pronounced like "evade"—also means "madness".'

His eyebrows shot up. 'Wait—what?! So I'm both wise *and* mad?'

'Yes,' I said with a smile. 'And honestly, you need a touch of madness to do anything exceptional. Steve Jobs once said: "Stay hungry, stay foolish." Hungry doesn't mean starving. It means having an inner fire, a drive to grow.'

'Okay ... and foolish?'

'Foolish doesn't mean dumb,' I said. 'It means being willing to take risks, to not always follow the crowd, to be curious enough to make mistakes and learn.'

'Hmm. But hunger and foolishness can look different for different people, right?'

'Exactly,' I said, smiling. 'For one person, hunger might be building a business. For another, it might be making music or serving society. For one, foolishness could be quitting a stable job to chase a dream. For another, it might simply be daring to say no when everyone expects a yes.'

'So my hunger might not be the same as my friend's?'

'Precisely. And here's the key—you can only know what kind of hunger and what kind of foolishness are right for you if you first know yourself. Otherwise, you'll end up chasing someone else's passion, someone else's dream, and mistake it for your own.'

Ved narrowed his eyes. 'Okay, but how do I know if it's *really* me, and not just me copying my friends? I mean, half the time we're all into the same stuff because everyone else is.'

I laughed. 'Great question. Think of it like a quick litmus test. There are three simple checks.'

'All right, hit me with the monk-approved checklist.'

'First,' I said, raising a finger, 'think about what you believe is right for you—your passion, your dream, your daily grind—and ask: Does it energize you or drain you? If it's truly your calling, it won't always be easy, but it will feel meaningful and give you energy.

'Second, does your passion last beyond the trend? If it excites you today but you're bored after a week, maybe it was just hype. But if the interest deepens the more you explore, then it's probably right for you.

'And third,' I added, 'would you still do it even if nobody noticed? If you'd enjoy it without applause, likes or validation, then your interest is authentic.'

Ved tapped his phone thoughtfully. 'Okay, so it's energy, endurance and no external approval. Got it.'

'You got it,' I said, smiling. 'That's how you know your hunger is real—and your foolishness is courage, not just imitation.'

I paused for a moment before adding, 'And remember, too much hunger without foolishness becomes blind ambition. Too much foolishness without hunger becomes recklessness. But together? That balance is what creates breakthroughs.'

Ved gave a quick laugh. 'Yeah ... my friend wants to drop out of engineering to start a company. His parents think he's nuts.'

I smiled knowingly. 'Maybe he is. But maybe that's his Ved moment—wisdom mixed with a little madness.'

For most of us, 'Stay hungry, stay foolish' won't mean starting the next breakthrough start-up, quitting our jobs overnight or chasing wild dreams without a safety net. Real life comes with responsibilities—bills to pay, families to care for, careers to build. Most of us will stay in our jobs, seek growth within them and carry financial and personal commitments alongside our ambitions.

But here's the point: Staying hungry and foolish isn't only about radical leaps—it's about everyday choices.

- Stay hungry in the everyday: This could mean staying curious in your role, learning new skills, pushing yourself to grow instead of slipping into comfort zones. It's the hunger to be a better leader, parent, partner or professional.
- Stay foolish in the everyday: This could mean daring to speak up in a meeting when everyone else is silent, trying out a new idea that might fail or saying 'no' to something that is misaligned with your values. Foolishness here is about courage in small, meaningful moments.

Breakthroughs don't always happen on magazine covers—they happen quietly, in the way you choose to live your daily life.

So the real question isn't: Will you risk it all for a dream?

The question is: Even within the boundaries of your reality, how can you keep your hunger alive and your foolishness courageous?

Ved looked out of the window, his features transforming into something softer. 'Yeah … maybe.'

For the first time, I could sense a subtle shift beneath his casual humour—a thought he wasn't ready to say out loud …

∼

By the time we neared the resort, the awkwardness brought about by our generation gap that I'd felt earlier had been somewhat bridged with laughter, curiosity and a shared moment of reflection.

And just before we pulled into the driveway of the flower-decked resort, Ved looked at me and said, 'You know, for someone in robes, you're kinda chill.'

'And for someone in an oversized hoodie, you're kinda wise,' I replied.

The car rolled to a stop, but I realized that a different kind of journey had already begun for Ved and me—and it can begin for each of us too, if only we choose to pause and make the effort to understand others, to understand ourselves and to understand our passion and purpose.

....

THINGS TO THINK ABOUT ...

SLAVERY VS SERVITUDE: True service, unlike slavery, is never imposed—it's a conscious act of love. When we release the need to control or command in our relationships and instead choose to contribute with care, something changes. Mutual respect replaces power struggles, and every bond begins to feel lighter, kinder and more alive.

THE THREE DIMENSIONS OF UNDERSTANDING: True harmony and growth come from mastering the art of understanding:
- Understanding others brings connection and harmony.
- Understanding ourselves brings clarity and balance.
- Understanding our passion gives us purpose.

HOW TO UNDERSTAND OTHERS: Two people can look at the same number—one sees a 6, the other a 9—and both are right from where they stand. The real shift comes when we walk around to see it from the other side, when we try to understand the 'why' behind the 'what'. Even if agreement never comes, understanding can. And often, understanding matters more than agreement.

How to Understand Ourselves—Pause, Reflect, Experiment:
- Pause: Step back from scrolling, running and reacting. Create space.
- Reflect: Ask yourself—What am I feeling right now? Why am I feeling it? What do I truly need?
- Experiment: Take small steps to meet the needs you uncover. Try new things. Notice what feels right and what doesn't.

How to Understand Our True Passion—The Litmus Test:
- Energy: Does it light you up and give you strength, or does it leave you feeling drained?
- Endurance: Does your interest stay alive beyond the trend, deepening with time?
- Authenticity: Would you still pursue it even if no one applauded, noticed or rewarded you?

The Balance of Hunger and Foolishness: Hunger without foolishness becomes blind ambition. Foolishness without hunger becomes recklessness. But together—hunger with courage—they become the spark of breakthroughs. And for most of us, staying hungry and foolish isn't about big risks—it's about the everyday decisions that keep us growing.

•••••••••••••••

The exercises related to the concepts mentioned in this chapter can be found on p. 255.

2

THE GAME OF SNAKES AND LADDERS

Navigating Failure and Finding True Success

~

Life's lessons come not in straight lines but in the ups and downs that shape who we become.

Arriving at the palace resort was nothing short of cinematic—it was as if a Bollywood set designer had swallowed a box of crayons, snorted some glitter and sneezed it all out in one glorious explosion.

Dhols and nagadas thundered so loudly I half-wondered whether they were announcing my arrival or starting a battle. Women in ghagra-cholis spun like whirlwinds of red, gold and turquoise. From the balconies above, rose petals rained down in slow motion. It was the kind of scene usually reserved for heroes making a dramatic entry in a film.

At the palace entrance stood a life-size cutout of the bride and groom, their smiles stretched as wide as their excitement. Guests lined up to click selfies with the cutout before entering the venue.

And then came Rakesh and his wife, Lakshmi. He looked every bit the successful patriarch—tall, broad-shouldered, his sherwani shimmering under the Rajasthan sun. She, in her soft pastel sari, was the quiet counterpoint: graceful, understated and effortlessly radiant. Their welcome was warm and personal—the kind that cut through the theatrics and reminded me why I was really there.

Just then, an attendant in a starched uniform appeared out of nowhere, bowing like I was royalty, and pressed a silver goblet into my hand. It was filled with something that sparkled suspiciously. It looked less like a drink and more like an audition prop for a luxury commercial.

'Swamiji, don't worry.' Rakesh laughed, catching my expression. 'It's just lemonade.'

'Good,' I joked, 'because if it was champagne, I'd end up saying my prayers in rhymes.'

As we entered the palace, the courteous hotel staff swooped in to take my faithful little carry-on, and Rakesh turned to me with his characteristic warmth.

'You must be tired, Swamiji. If you'd like, you can freshen up in your room and have lunch there quietly. Or,' he added with a smile, 'we haven't eaten yet either. It would make us very happy if you joined us. The chef has been briefed, and he has prepared a proper royal feast—tailored to your dietary preferences.'

I could sense that they genuinely wanted me to eat with them and, though I was a little tired, I agreed. Rest is important, but so is connection. Sometimes, rest is a genuine necessity and saying no is the obvious choice you can make for yourself. But then there are moments when braving a little tiredness is a small price to pay for shared warmth and togetherness. It's about learning when to say yes and when to say no—balance is the key.

I say this often these days, perhaps because so many of us are running faster than what our bodies, minds and hearts can keep up with. Dear friends, while saying *yes* can bring closeness, we must also learn the art of saying *no*—to protect our well-being. Sleep, rest and boundaries are not luxuries, they are essentials. Without them, we risk burning out and snapping at those we care about, all while running on an empty tank while pretending to be fine.

Whether it is giving ourselves to academics, work, relationships or even our own selves, we must remember that we live in a fast-paced world where keeping up puts a lot of pressure on us and leaves our minds unable to unwind, relax or simply take it easy. Resting our bodies and minds is critical to rebooting our systems.

But beyond caring for the body and mind, it's equally important to be with people who love us and wish us well—people whose presence doesn't drain our energy but restores it. That, too, is a kind of *emotional rest*—a safe space where we don't have to guard ourselves. Doing what we love—a hobby or even work aligned with our passion—even if it's hard work, still feels like rest, because it nourishes something deeper within. Trying to achieve these different kinds of rest regularly is what makes us feel fully human again.

I was once discussing this with a friend of mine, and he introduced me to a more structured version of this idea, one put forward by Dr Saundra Dalton-Smith. She says there are seven kinds of rest we all need.[1] The obvious one is *physical rest*—and it isn't just about sleep but also the kind of rest that comes from stretching, breathing deeply or simply letting the body be still. Then there's *mental rest*, that rare relief when the brain stops racing, and we no longer feel like we're juggling a thousand tabs all at once.

Next is *sensory rest*, because our senses, too, need rest—a holiday from screens, noise and bright lights, where silence itself feels like medicine. We also need *creative rest*—not by forcing ideas but by being surrounded with beauty and wonder until the imagination slowly wakes up again. *Emotional rest* comes when we can be honest without having to perform, when we can put down the heavy mask we carry for the world. *Social rest* is about choosing company that builds up your energy reserves instead of draining it—or sometimes choosing solitude without guilt. And finally, *spiritual rest*—the deepest of them all—that grounding sense of meaning and belonging that we touch in prayer, reflection, service or simply in gratitude.

Together, these seven types of rest form the foundation of true self-care. But in today's world, self-care is often misunderstood. It gets marketed as shutting everyone out, pampering ourselves endlessly or making 'me time' the only time. That isn't care, it is comfort turning into isolation.

Real self-care is different. It doesn't detach us from life; it equips us to participate in it more fully. It isn't an escape from responsibility—it's the fuel that helps us embrace responsibility with more energy and patience. It's not selfishness, it's stewardship—of the one mind and body we've been entrusted with.

The line, however, is delicate. Self-care becomes unhealthy when it slips into self-centredness—when every choice revolves around 'What about me?', and we stop asking, 'What about us?' That shift slowly severs us from the very thing that makes life rich: meaningful, loving connections.

True self-care is the pause that lets us breathe so we can listen better. It is the boundary that keeps us whole so we can give without resentment. It is the rest that restores us, not so we can retreat from others, but so we can return to them—lighter, calmer and more present.

And so I chose to accept Rakesh and Lakshmi's invitation to have lunch with them. Sometimes, nourishing the heart with company is as important as nourishing the body with food, rest and care.

I quickly freshened up and soon found myself walking into the palace restaurant with Rakesh, Lakshmi and Ved.

Now, this wasn't a restaurant—it was a chandelier showroom with tables. Crystal lights dangled from the ceiling, sparkling like constellations. The chairs were so ornate I felt guilty sitting on them, and the plates looked like they belonged in a museum rather than under dal and rice.

We settled into a quiet corner, away from the larger wedding crowd, and the servers glided in like perfectly choreographed dancers. The chef had indeed prepared what Rakesh had referred to as a royal feast—lavishly served yet thoughtfully tailored to my preferences. Dishes arrived one after another, placed with quiet precision: golden rotis that glistened with ghee, bowls of fragrant dal steaming gently, vegetables cooked with a subtle touch of spice, rice piled like a small white mountain and a tray of chutneys and pickles in jewel-like shades of green, red and gold.

Rakesh smiled and leaned closer. 'After consulting with Rohan and Sanjana, we decided to keep the wedding celebrations entirely vegetarian and alcohol-free. Everyone here is close family and friends, and we knew they'd understand and respect the thought behind it—to preserve the sanctity of the ceremonies and keep the focus where it belongs: on the marriage itself. Of course, for the grand reception in Mumbai, we'll make sure to cater to everyone's choices.'

I nodded, appreciating both the intention and the courage behind the decision. 'It's a beautiful thought,' I said. 'Society often forgets how to enjoy without dependence. To have fun without alcohol, talk without phones, love without conditions, dream without drugs and smile without posing for selfies—

these are joys in their purest form. And while I deeply respect each individual's personal choices, I also believe true happiness comes when we take charge of it ourselves, rather than making it the responsibility of something outside us.'

As we sat around the ornate table—Rakesh beside Lakshmi, with Ved and me across from them—sunlight streamed in through the window, catching the spark of wonder in Ved's young eyes.

The aroma of ghee and spices mingled with the sounds of laughter and the soft clinking of cutlery. And as we began to eat, the conversation soon became the real feast.

Ved leaned forward, elbows on the table. 'Gaurji, how do you know my nanu?'

Before I could respond, Rakesh spoke, 'I was on a flight about two years ago, when I happened to be seated next to Swamiji. We got talking and, at some point, he asked me my story.'

Ved's brows arched in surprise. 'And what's the story, Nanu?'

Rakesh's gaze softened. 'It was a long time ago … Back then, I was just a middle-class boy from Delhi with too many dreams and very few resources to make those dreams come true.'

'Really? You, Nanu?' Ved said, astonished. 'But look at you now—you live in a fancy home in one of the swankiest parts of Mumbai!'

Lakshmi chuckled. 'It's just a home, Vedu—not a palace like this. You're making us sound far grander than we really are.'

We laughed, Ved grinned and Rakesh continued, 'My father passed away when I was only ten. My mother—your great-grandmother, Rukmini Dadi—she did everything she could to raise me. Small domestic jobs, stitching, tutoring … She never let me feel we were broken, even when we were.'

Ved fell silent for a moment. When he spoke, his voice was raw with emotion. 'I didn't know that.'

'Behind every success, there's usually someone quietly holding things together,' I added softly. 'Someone who believes in you. Someone who wants you to succeed. Someone who takes joy in watching you grow. Such people are angels in our lives—because while the world often competes, they simply want us to rise. That's why I often say: "*Jo sukh mein saath dete hain unhe rishte kehte hain, lekin jo dukh mein saath dete hain unhe farishte kehte hain* [Those who stand by us in happiness are called relations, but those who stand by us in sorrow are called angels]." In your nanu's case, that angel was your Rukmini Dadi.'

Ved's eyes lit up. 'Wow, that farishte line is lit. So she's the real hero, isn't she?'

Rakesh smiled, his eyes moist. 'Yes, Vedu. She truly is. To help her, I started working too—delivering milk, newspapers, whatever came my way. Morning shifts before school, evening jobs after college. Survival leaves little room for choice.'

'Nanu, you delivered newspapers? Like … really carried them from house to house?'

'Of course.' Rakesh laughed. 'And trust me, those bundles weighed more than your schoolbag. My bicycle became my delivery van.'

'And you know how we met? Before our marriage, he'd come home to deliver newspapers—even in the rain, his clothes dripping wet, yet always smiling, as if it was just another part of the journey,' Lakshmi said softly.

Ved turned to her, eyes wide. 'And you still said yes to him?'

Lakshmi smiled shyly. 'I didn't marry him for his wet clothes. I married him for his warm heart.'

Rakesh shook his head. 'See, she always had a gentle heart.'

'That's so cheesy, Nani ...' Ved laughed. 'But kinda sweet too.'

Lakshmi laughed, her eyes wet. 'Cheesy or not, it's the truth.'

I was enjoying their sweet, loving banter as I listened to Rakesh's story—for the second time since our flight together. This time, it carried an even deeper meaning. It wasn't just a story of success, it was a quiet reminder of the power of sacrifice, responsibility, resilience and dedication—all anchored in love for the ones who mattered most to him. Stories often reveal new nuances when heard again—not because the words change, but because we do. The content doesn't change, but the context does—and the new context gives the same words new meaning. Each retelling of the story offers us a chance to hear what we may have missed before, to catch the subtler messages beneath the obvious ones.

There is a kind of wisdom that only lived experience can provide—wisdom that no self-help book, management degree or textbook can fully capture. Life's classroom doesn't come with a syllabus—its lessons are hidden in people, their choices, scars and laughter. That's why I love listening as much as I love speaking. Listening opens doors to fresher perspectives that no amount of solitary thinking can unlock.

We often underestimate it, but listening is an act of humility. It means admitting that someone else's journey holds treasures that we may not yet have found in our own. After all, don't they say, 'If you're the smartest person in the room, you're in the wrong room?' Every conversation is an invitation to learn, if we choose to quiet our own voice long enough to hear another's.

Someone very beautifully said:

> *Farak bahut hai aapki aur humari taleem mein,*
> *Aapne ustaadon se seekha hai, aur humne haalaaton se.*
>
> *There's a vast difference between your education and mine,*
> *You learned from teachers, while I learned from circumstances.*

Of course, we all learn from teachers. But let's not forget—we also learn from those whose only teachers were their struggles, those who carved out wisdom from pain. They become our teachers too. And in time, our own struggles shape us the same way, becoming silent lessons that we carry forward.

Rakesh's story was a gentle reminder that life is a never-ending curriculum, and wisdom is everywhere—if only we are willing to sit, listen and learn.

The butler reappeared discreetly, setting down a bowl of steaming curry, then slipping away without a word. The food accompanied the conversation like gentle background music—never overpowering, always enhancing.

Rakesh's tone grew serious again. 'After engineering, I worked a regular job for years, saved every rupee and bought a tiny house. That was my first step forward. Later, I started a small business—cables and wires. Honestly, I didn't think it would grow so much. But with hard work, sincerity, a little luck …'—he glanced at Lakshmi with a teasing smile—'and loads of Lakshmiji's blessings, we did well.'

She quickly shook her head. 'No, no. It was his dedication.'

I smiled. 'Every Rakesh needs his Lakshmi. Success may be earned, but stability is a gift.'

Ved blinked, trying to process it all. 'Wait, Nanu—I thought you were always like this,' he said, gesturing around at the grandeur of the wedding venue. 'You know … the fancy weddings, the big houses, all of it.'

Rakesh placed a hand on his grandson's shoulder. 'Never forget, Vedu—the beginning never defines the ending. I started with almost nothing. What matters is working with courage and never giving up.'

'And sometimes it's about waiting patiently, too—trusting that your time will come,' Lakshmi said.

Ved shook his head in disbelief. 'Nanu, you're cooler than I thought. Like … half-businessman, half-action-hero.'

I chuckled. 'And don't forget, full-time newspaper-delivery boy.'

Rakesh laughed, the weight of the memory mingling with pride. 'That's true. Those struggles shaped me. Without them, I wouldn't be who I am today.'

I nodded. 'Struggles aren't setbacks—they're the soil from which strength grows.'

By the time we finished talking, the butler returned with a small plate of desserts—kesari halwa glowing like liquid sunlight, rasmalai resting in creamy milk and rose petals, kulfi with delicate blossoms preserved in frozen condensed milk.

As I looked at the plate, I smiled. Struggles give life its depth, while sweetness makes it worth living. A meal ends beautifully with dessert, but a life finds its true beauty in lessons learned, love shared and connections cherished.

After lunch, as Rakesh, Lakshmi and Ved walked me to my room, we passed the palace garden. A little boy was darting across the lawn, chasing a yellow butterfly that danced just ahead of him. His tiny sandals slapped against the earth, his hair bouncing with every step, determination lighting up his face. But the more he tried to grab the butterfly, the higher and farther it flew, wings glinting in the sunlight.

'You see, Ved,' I said, pointing towards the boy, 'life's most precious things—success, love, peace, happiness—are like butterflies. The harder we chase them, the more they slip away. But if we create a beautiful garden through the right mindset, sincerity, hard work, kindness and good values, the butterflies will come to us on their own and stay. Chasing butterflies will leave you tired and empty-handed. But creating a garden brings not just one butterfly but many—and they'll return again and again.'

Isn't that true with our lives as well, friends?

How often do we chase butterflies in our own lives? We run after promotions, recognition, relationships or peace of mind with such intensity that we exhaust ourselves. We scroll endlessly for validation, we compare our journey with others, we push ourselves harder and harder—yet the very things we crave keep slipping away.

But think of the times when you weren't chasing anything. When you were absorbed in your work, giving your best with sincerity. When you invested in relationships with kindness, without expecting anything back. When your actions were shaped by your values, and not the pressure you faced. Wasn't it in those moments that success found you? That love deepened? That peace quietly settled in your heart?

That's the power of building a garden. A garden doesn't demand attention from butterflies—it simply becomes so inviting that the butterflies choose it. In the same way, when we focus on creating an environment of growth, learning, sincerity and service, the things we long for begin to show up naturally. Success comes as a recognition of effort. Love comes as a reflection of care. Peace comes as the by-product of living in alignment with our values and purpose.

I smiled and turned back to Rakesh. 'You built such a garden. And that's why your life is filled with butterflies.'

Rakesh nodded quietly. 'That's true, Swamiji. I never really chased wealth or success. I just tried to live by certain values, work hard and be sincere. Maybe that's why life gave me more than I ever imagined.'

Lakshmi, who had been listening silently, said, 'And gardens need patience too, Vedu. You can't plant seeds today and expect flowers tomorrow.'

Ved grinned. 'Yeah! So Nanu didn't chase success—he just built the vibe, and success showed up on its own.'

We all laughed, the image of butterflies still lingering in my mind as we reached my suite.

The first time in my life someone told me, 'You'll be staying in a suite,' I was confused. Sweet, I thought, that's something you eat after a meal. Then they showed me the spelling—suite. I frowned. English really does like playing tricks on us.

The suite they had reserved for me here was elegant, spacious and warm. There was a comfortable living area with an ornate table that seemed to invite me to set up my little worship altar for the morning puja. Beyond the large windows, a small backyard opened up to a pond dotted with lilies, bees flitting around them. I immediately thought that this was the perfect spot for my morning chanting and meditation.

Rakesh smiled, noticing my quiet appreciation. 'We chose this suite for you because it's in a secluded corner of the resort. The wedding crowd won't be coming up this way. You'll have privacy for your prayers, and at the same time, you can step in and out of the festivities whenever you wish.'

It felt like the best of both worlds—solitude when I needed it, and the privilege to join in whenever I wished to.

The suite was indeed an ideal setting for my sadhana—my daily spiritual practice. For me, it isn't just a ritual, it's my lifeline. If I am like an electric bulb, then sadhana is the cable that connects me to the source of positivity, strength, joy and peace. Puja, or worship, makes that connection even more personal—when I make a simple offering of flowers or incense to my beloved deities, I am plugging my heart back into the divine source.

My mission is to serve others—to share, to give, to contribute. But even a well, if it keeps giving without being refilled, will eventually run dry. A spiritual practice keeps the well connected to the unlimited ocean—that reservoir which never runs out.

And sadhana is not just for monks. In fact, it is even more necessary for those living lives of non-stop giving—parents giving to children, families giving to each other, professionals giving to their work, caregivers giving to those in need. Love, hope, support, resources, time, space—we keep pouring it all out. But if we never refill our reserves, we run the risk of exhaustion, of burning out.

That's why spiritual practice is not a privilege—it's a necessity. By connecting to the ocean of divinity, we keep our wells full. And when our wells are full, we can keep giving, without drying up and without being overdependent on others to fill them.

As I settled into my room, Ved's sharp eyes immediately landed on a familiar box kept neatly on a side table.

'Gaurji!' he exclaimed, lifting it up. 'This is my favourite game—Snakes and Ladders! My friends and I play it all the time on my iPad. We all love it. Can we play this, please?'

Rakesh and Lakshmi exchanged a glance. They had been urging me to rest after the long journey, but they also saw what was unfolding—a sweet, respectful bond forming between a Gen Z teenager and a Gen X monk in such a short span of time. I knew they wanted Ved to have this moment of joy and gentle mentoring.

I smiled. 'I would surely love to rest ... and I will. But only after a game. Let's all play one round together.'

Ved's face lit up instantly. Rakesh chuckled and Lakshmi shook her head with a smile that meant she had already given in.

Snakes and Ladders is one of the oldest and simplest board games in the world. Each player has a token, and you move it forward depending on what the dice says. Ladders give you a shortcut ahead, while snakes send you sliding back down. The first one to reach the very last square wins.

It sounds simple enough, but anyone who has played the game knows that things can get dramatic. One moment you're leading the board, the next a snake swallows you whole and you're back where you started. Dice are slammed, mock arguments break out and some even try blowing on the dice for extra luck. And yet, no matter how many times you lose, you still want to roll again.

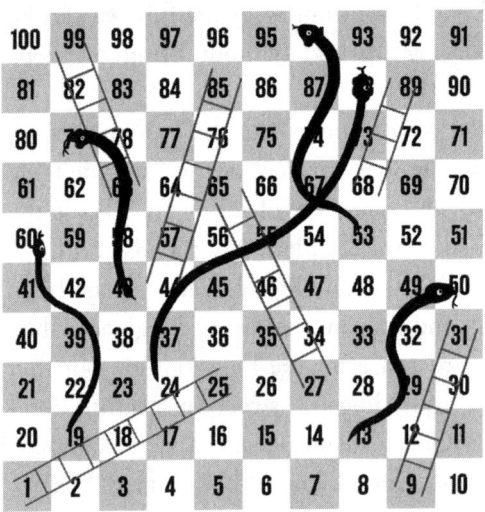

The board was laid out on the ornate table and the tokens lined up neatly at the starting square: Ved picked green, Rakesh chose red, Lakshmi took blue and I was left with orange.

Ved smirked instantly. 'Of course, orange for Gaurji. Monk colour! Even the board knows your brand.'

We all burst out laughing before the dice had been rolled even once.

Ved went first, naturally. 'The youngest should always start,' he declared with full confidence. He shook the dice with exaggerated flair, blew on it like it was a birthday candle and rolled a six.

'See!' Ved jumped up as if he'd just conquered the world. 'Didn't I tell you? I'm the master of this game!'

Rakesh rolled next and got a two. He sighed dramatically, throwing up his hands. 'Even in retirement, I'm working overtime. Always behind!'

'Oi,' I said, smiling, 'you're just pacing yourself wisely.'

My turn came, and I rolled a three. 'Slow and steady,' I said, moving my token.

Lakshmi's first roll landed her at the bottom of a ladder, and she climbed up.

Ved immediately groaned. 'Nani, this isn't fair!'

Rakesh chuckled. 'That's your nani, Vedu. She wins quietly.'

On his next roll, Ved landed on a snake's head and slid down. He crossed his arms. 'This game is biased. The dice hates me!'

I laughed. 'Ah, Ved—that's classic human tendency. When things go our way, we call it skill. When they don't, we call it unfair.'

Rakesh nodded knowingly. 'True. When my first business deal collapsed, I blamed the market, my partner, even the weather. It took years for me to realize it wasn't any of this—it was me, I was unprepared.'

Ved blinked. 'So if I keep blaming the dice, I'll never win?'

'Exactly,' I said. 'The dice is never in our control. But what we do with the roll—that's always in our hands.'

'And sometimes, Ved,' Lakshmi said, 'it's not even about winning. It's about enjoying the game with the people you're playing with.'

A few turns later, I landed on a fat grinning snake and slid far down.

Ved leapt up in delight. 'Finally! Even monks get bitten!'

Rakesh laughed. 'See? Life is fair after all.'

I smiled. 'Yes, snakes don't spare anyone. But it doesn't mean that the game has come to an end. The snakes remind us that no matter how low we fall, we must always be ready to start again.'

Ved soon hit a ladder and zoomed ahead. 'Shortcut, baby!' he declared.

Lakshmi smiled. 'Careful. Sometimes ladders only bring you closer to a snake.'

I added, 'Ladders lift us, yes, but they also test us. They check if our head spins with pride.'

Later, I too landed at the foot of a tall ladder and climbed up quickly.

As we neared the top of the board, the tension grew. Ved was at 84, Rakesh at 87, Lakshmi at 93, while I trailed at 76.

Ved whispered prayers and rolled. The dice landed ... right on the head of a monster snake at 88. Down he went, sliding all the way back to 24.

Ved clutched his head. 'Nooo! Everyone's climbing. I'm the only one falling!'

'Ved,' I chuckled, 'that's how life feels sometimes. It seems like the whole world is rising up while you're the only one sliding down. But one roll changes everything.'

He collapsed on the carpet. 'I was so close. This sucks!'

Rakesh roared with laughter. 'Blockbuster moment! The hero falls in the last act. Perfect climax!'

Lakshmi shook her head with a patient smile. 'Ved, it's only a game.'

Ved sat up, still melodramatic. 'Game? No, Nani. This is *Toofaan*. My dreams just got punched in the face.'

I leaned in. 'You know, Ved, you're not wrong. Your snake at 88 is exactly like Aziz Ali, the character Farhan Akhtar played so brilliantly in *Toofaan*. Remember the final fight? He's bruised, battered, his body ready to give up. His mind whispers, It's over. His shoulders sag, his guard drops. Just like yours did after that snake.'

'Oh yeah …' Ved said, 'and then his coach shouts: "Do it for her!"'

'And suddenly,' I continued, 'it's not about the title any more. It's about his wife—his *why*. It's about love, purpose, redemption. That one reminder changes everything. His legs become steady, his fists tighten. Pain doesn't vanish, but it loses its power.'

Ved gripped the dice. 'So this snake is my knockout punch. And rolling again is me … going another round?'

I nodded. 'Life will throw snakes, punches and setbacks your way. The dice may feel unfair. But the real question is: Why do you keep rolling?'

Ved thought for a moment, then smiled. 'Fine. I'll roll again. But this time, I'm doing it for Nani. She deserves to see me win.'

Lakshmi laughed warmly. Rakesh gave a mock warrior cheer. And I nodded. 'That's it, Ved. Even in Snakes and Ladders, your why keeps you rolling. In life too, purpose—love, family, faith, service—is what makes us pick up the dice again after every fall.'

Ved raised his fist dramatically. 'One more round!'

The tokens glided, the dice rattled, the laughter echoed. And beneath all the noise, life whispered its truth: Snakes test your patience. Ladders test your pride. But your why? It tests your heart—and when it's strong enough, you'll always keep rolling.

Once the game was over and the tokens were packed back into the box, Ved leaned back with a grin that mixed pride and relief.

'Gaurji, thank you for this,' he said. 'It was fun. The lessons too.'

'Learning wrapped in laughter always goes deeper. And by the way ... here's a fun fact.'

Ved raised an eyebrow. 'Here we go ... spiritual gyan incoming.'

Lakshmi laughed. 'Shh, let him finish. I love these nuggets.'

Rakesh nodded. 'Me too.'

I continued, 'The game of Snakes and Ladders actually has a surprisingly deep and spiritual origin. It didn't begin as entertainment but as a teaching tool for philosophy, morality and self-realization.

'In ancient India, it was called Moksha Patam—the ladder to salvation.[2] Saints designed it to teach karma and dharma. Ladders stood for virtues like truth, compassion and devotion—they lifted the soul upwards. Snakes stood for vices like greed, anger and pride—they dragged the soul down. And the final square? Moksha. Liberation from the cycle of birth and death.'

Lakshmi's eyes sparkled. 'How beautiful! Every move is a reminder of life itself.'

I added, 'The lesson was simple—life has ladders as well as snakes. Your choices determine where you end up. But no matter how many times you fall, you always get another chance to roll.'

'Exactly what I keep telling you, Vedu. Never give up,' Rakesh said.

Ved smiled. 'Fine, fine. The moral of the story is: Snakes are bad, ladders are good, and I always win.'

As I walked them to the door, Lakshmi spotted someone outside and called out, 'Priya!'

A graceful woman turned and immediately walked over. Rakesh's face lit up. 'Gaurji, this is our daughter, Priya,' he said warmly. 'She's a talented fashion designer doing remarkable work in Mumbai.'

Lakshmi placed a hand on her arm and added, 'Yes, she's truly carved her own path. We're so proud of her.'

Ved jumped in, unable to resist. '*Aakhir mummy kiski hai* [Whose mother is she, after all]?' he teased, clearly enjoying his own line. Our laughter echoed in the corridor.

Priya accepted the praise with a polite smile. 'I'm just trying to do my bit,' she said gently. She spoke little, but her presence carried a quiet strength and an effortless grace.

Rakesh looked at her with a fondness that was unmistakable. Lakshmi beamed with pride. Ved leaned into Priya's side with easy sweetness, as only children can. But as Rakesh held her gaze a moment longer, I noticed a faint shadow in Priya's eyes—the kind that appears when joy brushes against an old memory.

Nothing more was said, but in that moment I sensed that familiar truth about families—beneath every laugh, there are also quiet, unspoken emotions. Some things are celebrated, others are carried silently, until the time is right to share them.

∼

Later, alone in my room, I found myself reflecting on how my social media journey had been nothing less than a game of Snakes and Ladders.

When I first started posting on social media, it felt like I was rolling the dice without knowing the rules. Some posts barely moved a few steps forward. Others, unexpectedly, caught people's attention and it felt like a ladder was propelling me upwards. One video would suddenly be shared everywhere and I'd think, 'This is it, I've made it to 99!' But then … silence. A snake. Viewer engagement would drop, criticism would creep in, and I'd find myself back on square 10, wondering if I should keep playing at all.

Of course, my intention was always to share wisdom and spread the message. Yet, like in the game itself, the snakes and ladders do affect you—they remind you that while the dice may not always be in your control, your purpose can be.

The truth is, both snakes and ladders are part of the game. You can't enjoy the thrill of the ladders without letting the snakes humble you. And the biggest lesson is that neither define you—the dice keeps rolling as long as you keep showing up.

For me, the ladders came when I spoke authentically, when I shared stories straight from my heart. The snakes appeared whenever I tried too hard to please the algorithms, trends or expectations. Each snake taught me humility while each ladder taught me gratitude. And both together taught me perseverance.

The greatest anchor for me was a principle explained by Shri Krishna in the Bhagavad Gita—Nishkama Karma Yoga. It involves working with attachment but disconnecting with detachment.

Nishkama Karma means giving our best without being attached to the result. It's not about being lazy or careless—it's about doing our duty with sincerity and then letting go. If there's no passion, we stop trying. But if we're too attached, we suffer when things don't go our way. The dice won't always roll in our favour, and that's when detachment helps us stay calm, accept what comes with grace and dignity, and try again.

And then there is the danger of getting carried away by two extremes—ladders that feed our ego and snakes that fuel our hopelessness. We swing endlessly between pride and despair. Even Arjun, the great warrior of the Mahabharata, felt that pull on the battlefield—torn between duty and emotion, clarity and confusion.

Nishkama Karma teaches us equanimity—to stay balanced. Yes, as humans, we will get affected. But the practice helps us bounce back quicker, and with grace. My years of ashram training, before I ever touched social media, were invaluable in helping me navigate this game.

And here's the key: Nishkama Karma becomes Yoga when we tie our work to something higher. When our actions are not just for personal gain but are offered in service—to others, to society or to the Divine—they carry a deeper purpose. Then every effort, whether big or small, becomes sacred. Writing a post, preparing a meal, helping a colleague, raising a child—any of it can become Yoga if done in the spirit of contribution.

When we work this way, ladders don't inflate our ego because we see them as grace, and snakes don't crush our spirit because we see them as growth. Both become part of a larger journey of service.

So how can you bring this into your life? By practising Nishkama Karma Yoga in three simple steps:

1. **Effort (Give Your Best)**: Show up fully in whatever you do—your work, your relationships, your growth. Passion and discipline matter.
2. **Detachment (Release the Outcome)**: Once you've done your best, let go of the obsessive grip on results. The odds won't always be in your favour—and that's okay. Detachment helps you accept success with humility and failure with dignity.
3. **Service (Tie It to Something Higher)**: Karma becomes Yoga when we connect our actions to service—to others, to society or to the Divine. Every act, big or small, can be an offering if done in the spirit of contribution.

So if you're chasing a dream—whether it's social media growth, a career milestone or a personal goal—remember this: It's not about reaching the hundredth square in one perfect roll. It's about staying in the game, learning from every climb and every fall, and remembering that every square you land on is shaping you.

Because in the end, life isn't about avoiding snakes. It's about learning to rise again, roll again and keep moving—until your story finds its way to others.

My mind wandered back to Rakesh's story—how he had lost his father very early in life and how, as a young boy, he stood by his mother, helping her run the household by taking up small jobs while pursuing his education. Over the years, through grit and perseverance, he rose to become the successful industrialist he is today—with affluence, influence and a home filled with love and warmth.

Often, we only see the tip of the iceberg—the visible success, the achievements, the life people have built. What we fail to notice is the vast part beneath the surface, hidden from the eyes—failures, disappointments, struggles, commitment, discipline and resilience—that truly holds everything up.

Life is unpredictable—there are sudden rises, unexpected falls, twists we never see coming. Outcomes are often shaped by forces beyond our control, but what truly defines the journey is how we respond—the effort we make, the resilience we cultivate and the purpose we hold close. Setbacks teach us humbling lessons, and opportunities open doors to growth. Progress is never linear; it unfolds as a rhythm of advances and retreats, pauses and leaps, each shaping us into who we are meant to become.

And if we wish to manifest the life we dream of, it is not luck we must chase, but the discipline of staying with the process—showing up, step after step, until success reveals itself.

With these reflections still echoing in my mind, I let myself pause—a brief rest before the evening activities began.

....

THINGS TO THINK ABOUT ...

HOW TO MANIFEST WHAT WE WANT—BUTTERFLY WISDOM: Success, love, peace and happiness are like butterflies. The harder we chase them, the farther away they fly. But when we create a garden filled with sincerity, kindness and purpose, they come and stay.

SPIRITUAL PRACTICE IS NOT A PRIVILEGE—IT'S A NECESSITY: Spiritual practice is not just for monks. It is even more vital for those living lives of constant giving. When we're connected to the divine source, our inner wells stay nourished. And when we're full, we can keep giving—without running on an empty tank or relying on others to fill us up.

SNAKES AND LADDERS—RESILIENCE IN SUCCESS AND FAILURE:
- Rolling the dice is in our control, but the number it'll stop at isn't. Doing our best is in our hands, the rest is destiny.
- Fortunes can change quickly—one moment we're ahead, the next we're sliding back. Let's stay humble when we rise and determined when we fall.
- Snakes don't spare anyone, but they don't end the game either. They remind us that no matter how high we climb or how far we slide, we must always be ready to begin again.
- The human tendency is to blame luck when we fail and take credit for ourselves when we succeed. Instead of blaming or boasting, just keep rolling.
- The journey matters as much as the win—the real joy is in playing together.
- When setbacks knock us down, it's purpose that gives us the strength to stand up and roll again.

NISHKAMA KARMA YOGA: The Gita reminds us that we must do our best to detach from the outcome and connect our work to something higher—be it service to others or to the Divine. This is how an ordinary action becomes sacred, and how we can stay balanced regardless of whether life gives us ladders or snakes.

LIFE IS UNPREDICTABLE, WITH SUDDEN RISES AND UNEXPECTED FALLS: What shapes our journey most isn't the outcome, but the effort we bring to it and the intention that guides us. Results are often influenced by forces outside our reach, yet our response—to triumphs, setbacks and pauses along the way—defines our growth. Progress never follows a straight line; it moves in cycles of rise and fall, each turn refining who we are becoming.

●●●●●●●●●●●●●●●●

The exercises related to the concepts mentioned in this chapter can be found on p. 262.

3

CRACKED MUGS

Finding Beauty and Acceptance in Imperfection

~

The cracks in our lives are not failures—they are stories etched in gold, waiting to unfold.

In the evening, the palace came alive with the arrival of the guests. Cars rolled in through the arched driveway, their headlights cutting briefly across the sandstone walls before vanishing into the dusk. Porters in crisp uniforms hurried to unload luxury suitcases, their gleaming metal name-tags catching the light of the lanterns that had just been lit along the pathway.

Inside, the high-ceilinged lobby echoed with a mix of sounds—warm greetings, bursts of laughter, the rustle of silk saris and tailored suits brushing against each other. A few of Rohan's closest friends staked out a corner near the reception desk, joking with each other. Rakesh and Lakshmi's relatives and family friends mingled nearby, exchanging handshakes, hugs and smiles that carried decades of shared history.

Sanjana's side of the gathering was smaller, more understated. Apart from Gaurav—her brother and only family present—she had only a few friends with her. Their presence by her side was steady, like a gentle anchor in the swirl of the festivities.

The guest list was intimate—only about forty people in all. Yet the atmosphere was anything but modest. Bellboys wheeled food trolleys across marble floors that glittered under golden chandeliers. Silver trays of welcome drinks drifted through the crowd, the clink of glasses punctuating the evening chatter. And out on the terrace, a Rajasthani musician drew his bow across a sarangi, its soulful notes rising into the desert air.

Guided by the music and the fragrance of spices in the air, the gathering slowly moved towards the palace's terrace restaurant. There we found the heart of the celebration—the air was electric with soft laughter, music and the glow of a hundred lanterns swaying gently in the desert breeze. Above, the full moon hung radiant, casting its silver light across the sand dunes that stretched endlessly into the horizon.

I arrived quietly into this warmth. Since lunch had been heavy and late, I preferred to skip dinner, but Rakesh wouldn't let me slip past unnoticed. With his usual courteousness, he took me around, introducing me personally to his relatives and guests and eventually Rohan and Sanjana. I had met Rohan just once before—a brief, formal exchange. But this was my first meeting with Sanjana. She carried herself with quiet grace, her smile modest, her eyes alive with the kind of happiness that makes words unnecessary. Rakesh then guided me to a quieter table in one corner of the terrace. 'You'll be comfortable here,' he said warmly, before he and Lakshmi returned to the rhythm of hosting, greeting and making every guest feel seen.

Just as the plates began to be cleared, one of Rohan's friends stood up and tapped his glass. 'All right, for those who don't know me,' he began, grinning, 'I had the privilege—or should I say misfortune—of spending three years with this guy at King's College in London.' A ripple of laughter rolled across the tables. 'That's where he met Sanjana. Or should I say, where she tolerated him long enough to realize he was worth keeping?'

The merry toast continued on—stories of their student days in London, late-night study sessions that turned into midnight feasts, jokes about Rohan's cooking skills (or the lack of them) and recollections of how Sanjana always managed to top every exam without looking like she even tried. The evening grew lighter and brighter with every quip, the terrace now filled not just with music but with a shared joy that knit friends and families together.

I was content in my quiet corner, sipping water and soaking in the atmosphere, when Priya appeared. A little hesitant, she asked me softly, 'If it's not too much of a disturbance, may I join you?'

I smiled. 'Oh, it's no disturbance at all. You're more like a rescue mission for a monk stranded at a party, who's not quite sure what he's meant to do.'

She chuckled. It was just the right icebreaker for a first-time conversation.

We began to talk. She thanked me for befriending her son, Ved. 'It's not easy,' she said, shaking her head. 'Nineteen, Gen Z and full of opinions. He's a hard one to reach sometimes.'

I laughed. 'True. But every generation thinks the other is impossible. You know how it is, right? *Ghar ki kheer, dal barabar.* Parents give the sweetest advice, but kids dismiss it like it's plain dal. And honestly, if parents say it, it's boring. But if someone else says the same thing, suddenly, it's wisdom. I'm just cashing in on that unfair rule! The real trick isn't lectures—it's listening and showing empathy without judgement. That's when kids like Ved begin to open up. So it's not really about me, it's just about an outside voice sometimes.'

She nodded, her expression softening, as if a small burden had been lightened. Then, leaning in a little, she asked with curiosity, 'So what about you? Tell me about your life.'

I smiled. 'Oh, nothing much—just some travels here and there, a few speaking engagements, some writing, the usual monk routine.' I waved it off lightly, and then turned the question back to her. 'But enough about me. What about you? I heard you're a fashion designer?'

A waiter passed nearby, and Priya lifted her hand slightly. 'Could I have a coffee, please?' she said, before turning back to me with a faint, almost-fragile smile.

She spoke as though she was speaking out her thoughts as they came to her. 'Designing outfits that make others look beautiful ... But what does it really do for someone like me?' Her eyes dropped for a moment. She wasn't fishing for compliments—it felt deeper, like a confession that had slipped out.

I didn't answer right away. As a monk, I had learned that silence often speaks louder than words—a quiet reassurance that says, I'm here to understand, not to fix.

'It's hard to even say this ... because it feels like I'm reliving my childhood all over again,' she continued, her voice catching. 'My father, Rakeshji. A successful businessman, noble, respected, generous to so many. And yet ...' Her words faltered. She stared at the lantern on the table, its flame shivering in the desert breeze—weak and unsteady, like the tremor in her voice.

'They say "*diya tale tale andhera*" [darkness under the lamp],' she whispered, her lips curling into a bitter smile. 'For the world, he was all light. With me ... he was neglectful, uncaring, unloving. Why? Because I wasn't like the rest of the Aroras. I was darker in complexion. Not fair like my parents or my brother, Rohan. Not great at academics. Overweight.'

Just then, the waiter returned, setting a steaming cup of coffee before Priya. She wrapped her hands around it, clinging to its warmth. Her eyes had a faraway look, lost in the weight of what she was remembering.

'And slowly, his indifference convinced me that I was less. Not enough. Undeserving of the warmth others received so easily.'

From the far side of the terrace came the chime of glasses and the rise of a folk song. But here, in this quiet corner, Priya's words lingered in the air like echoes across empty dunes.

'Mom tried,' she continued, 'but her voice was too small in our household. I turned to art—it was the only place where I felt ... like myself. That's how I found fashion. Dad resisted even that, but when he saw I had nothing else, he grudgingly allowed it.'

She stirred the coffee absently, even though she hadn't added any sugar. Then she lifted the cup and took a slow sip.

'At the first design firm where I worked, I met Vinay.' A faint smile touched her lips. 'He was tall, fair, dynamic— everything I thought I wasn't. I was his assistant designer. Somehow ... he saw me. Not my complexion, my weight, my flaws—just me.' She looked down into her cup. 'I once told him I felt unworthy of him. He laughed and said, "That's your story, not mine." He never let me feel less. Not even once.'

I stayed silent, letting her words find their space in the night air.

'When we wanted to marry, Dad resisted again. Mom fought for me. And Vinay ... he built me a life. We started our own label, and we thrived. Then Ved was born.' Her face brightened for a moment. 'For the first time, life felt like a painting—vibrant and complete ... And then ...' her voice wavered, 'after we moved into the new house that Vinay had built for us, when Ved was just two ...' She stopped, her lips trembling. 'He collapsed ... right there ... in front of me. Cardiac arrest. And then ... he was gone. Gone in my arms.'

The sarangi on the far terrace played a note so aching it seemed to feel her pain.

I said nothing. Just sat with her, so her grief could find its way through.

After a long pause, she spoke again. Her voice was stripped of all strength. 'Dad has been supportive since then. He adores Ved. Maybe it's his way of making up for what he didn't give me. But that doesn't change what I lost—my childhood, my self-worth … and Vinay.' She looked at me, eyes brimming with tears. 'Even now, I feel unworthy. Less. Incomplete. I don't know how to deal with it.'

I decided to not respond right away.

How does one react when someone shares their life story and pours out their pain in front of you?

Most of us feel the urge to fix it. To say something that will make the other person feel instantly better. Some try to give advice, others distract with humour, a few change the subject entirely. We do this not because we don't care, but because we are uncomfortable with pain—both theirs and our own.

But here is the paradox: When someone is pouring out their heart, they are not necessarily asking for a solution. They are asking for space. They don't need us to rush to 'make it better'. They need our patience to 'let it be'.

Think of a candle in a dark room. It doesn't chase the darkness away—it simply shines, quietly, helping others find their way and see what's around them again. In the same way, when someone shares their pain, our role isn't to fight their darkness but to stay beside them until their light returns.

Silence, then, is not emptiness but presence. A silence filled with compassion can heal more deeply than a thousand words of hurried advice. When we resist the urge to interrupt, analyse, compare with our own stories, we give the other person the rare gift of feeling *heard*.

So the next time someone sits across from you, holding back tears, let your heart say what your lips don't need to: I am here. I am with you. I don't have to fix you. I just want to be with you. That, more than anything else, is what allows a broken spirit to begin healing.

And that is what I tried to do with Priya.

~

She reached again for her coffee, her hands still trembling. The cup slipped against the saucer with a sharp sound. She caught it quickly, but not before a thin crack ran along the rim.

For a moment, she just stared at it. It was no ordinary cup—delicate porcelain, ivory white with faint blue vines curling along its surface, the kind of piece chosen to match the grandeur of the palace setting. The crack looked almost out of place on something so carefully crafted.

'Even this cup ... it looks fine on the outside, but once it's cracked, people usually throw it away. That's how I feel. Presentable to the world but broken inside. It's been seventeen years since Vinay's gone,' she said, the number heavy on her tongue. 'I've managed ... with work, with Ved. On the outside, I look like I've coped well. And in some ways, I have.' She paused. 'But inside ... the old traumas still linger. I still feel the same sense of being unworthy or incomplete. Like, no matter what I build, some part of me still crumbles.'

She looked up at me then, her eyes searching. 'I know this is a sensitive topic, and I can see you're careful not to just ... pounce in with advice. And I respect that.' Her lips curved into a faint smile. 'But honestly, Swamiji, I'm giving you full licence here. Please, share your thoughts and ideas. I promise not to sue you if they don't work.' She chuckled at her own line. 'Besides, if a monk can't say something wise over coffee, then who can?'

I smiled. 'Sue me? That would be the first time a monk ends up in court for giving free advice. I'll have to start carrying a legal disclaimer along with my robes: "Warning—may cause unsolicited wisdom."'

Her laughter broke through, softening the discomfort in the air.

I spoke again, my tone softer now. 'But thank you, Priya ... for trusting me enough to ask. Seventeen years is not a short journey. You've carried work, motherhood and responsibility with dignity. Yet I also hear the part of you that still feels the old wounds, the unworthiness, the incompleteness. And I want you to know—it makes complete sense. Some traumas don't vanish just because time passes. They leave marks, just like the crack on this cup. But a crack doesn't mean you're broken beyond use. It only means you've lived and experienced more than most could.'

She looked at me and waited for me to continue speaking.

'Priya ...' I said, 'there are many ways I could respond to your situation. But your cracked coffee cup reminded me of another story. It is about Meera, a member of our community in Mumbai, who often attended my talks at the ashram.

'After one session, where I had spoken about how the universe sends us signs just when we need them, she shared something remarkable. Earlier that very day, her mug had slipped, leaving behind a fine hairline crack. And later, almost as if by design, she stumbled upon an ancient and empowering art form called Kintsugi.[1]

'Now, whether you call this observation, memory and recall, coincidence, destiny, or just a monk trying to make up tales over coffee—here's the story …'

And so I shared Meera's experience with Priya. And dear friends, I share it with you too. Maybe it will make you reflect on what you believe are your own cracks, your own inadequacies, your own stories—and help you find meaning in them.

∽

On a Tuesday morning, the mug broke. Not in a dramatic, clattering fall—just a soft thud on the kitchen counter, and a quiet hairline crack ran through the side of her favourite ceramic mug. The one Meera had bought ten years ago at a small artisan stall in Jaipur. Handmade. Slightly asymmetrical. The glaze uneven in places. A pale blue swirl at the bottom, like a lazy ocean wave.

She could've thrown it away. Instead, she sat down, fingers running along the crack. She was strangely moved by it. Maybe because she felt cracked herself.

Meera was fifty-two. And lately, she had started noticing herself more in mirrors and less in photographs.

Her once thick black hair had turned salt and pepper—more salt than pepper these days. A small pouch of stubborn fat clung to her lower belly. There were lines around her eyes, near her lips and along the gentle sag of her neck that she tried not to look at while brushing her teeth.

Once upon a time, she would've considered herself beautiful. Sharp-featured, slim, graceful. But now, beauty had quietly left the room, like a guest who didn't say goodbye.

She sighed and sipped her tea—still warm, still comforting. The mug held it just fine.

Maybe she was like the mug, she thought.

At work, things weren't encouraging either. She had been a copywriter for over twenty years. Words were her forte. But lately, the young ones—with their fresh tattoos, quick wit and caffeinated vocabulary—seemed to run laps around her.

She wasn't jealous. Not really.

She was just … tired. And sometimes she felt a little invisible. Her ideas were still good, but they came in slower. She triple-checked her emails before sending them. And she often deleted clever lines because they read too much like 'someone trying to sound clever'.

The previous week, her manager had smiled and said, 'You're the emotional depth of this team, Meera.'

She wasn't sure if it was a compliment or a hint at retirement.

In her relationships, the silence had grown louder.

Her husband, Rajeev, was kind. Safe. They shared a home, bills, the remote control. And some evenings, during dinner, they even shared a silence that was companionable rather than awkward. But gone were the days of passionate debates, spontaneous laughter or late-night foot rubs.

They spoke in updates now:

'Milk's over.'

'Your sister called.'

'The plumber's coming at four.'

Once, their relationship had been poetic. Now, it was a to-do list.

Her daughter, Tara, lived in London. The time difference had become an excuse more than a hurdle. Texts had replaced calls. Emojis had replaced emotion.

'Miss you, Ma 🖤,' Tara would send.

Meera would reply, 'Miss you too, beta 💕'—and then stare at the chat screen, hoping for more words that never came.

But then, one Sunday, something shifted.

She was scrolling mindlessly when she stumbled across a video of a Japanese artist repairing broken pottery with gold. It was an art form called Kintsugi, which repaired broken pottery with lacquer rather than tossing out the piece.

'Because,' the artist said softly, 'what breaks becomes more beautiful if you let it.'

Meera paused the video, replayed that line and sat with it.

Over the next few days, she looked at her life through that golden lens.

Her face? Lived in. A map of every smile and season.

Her body? It had carried a child, endured a surgery, danced under monsoon skies and stood for hours at the stove, cooking for the whole family during festivals.

Her career? Sure, she wasn't viral on social media, but she had once written an ad that made a client cry in gratitude and joy. And it stayed with people longer than a tweet ever could.

Her marriage? It wasn't fireworks. But it was shelter. And peace. And on difficult days, Rajeev still remembered how she liked her tea—ginger, no sugar, extra hot.

So she started making small changes.

She stopped hiding her greys and tied her hair into a silver bun.

She wore a sari that had a stain near the pallu. 'This is from when I dropped chutney laughing too hard at my niece's joke,' she told someone at a family dinner. 'Good memory.'

She sent her daughter a voice note instead of a text. 'No pressure to reply,' she said. 'Just wanted you to hear my voice.'

She even told her junior colleague at work, 'I don't always have quick ideas, but I do have deep ones—if you ever want to bounce thoughts off a slow thinker.'

One evening, Rajeev looked up from his newspaper and said, 'You're ... lighter these days. Did something change?'

Meera smiled. 'Nothing. Everything.'

He nodded. 'I like it.'

She liked it too.

On her fifty-third birthday, she repaired the cracked mug with a DIY gold paint pen. Not real gold, but enough to make the crack glitter.

When her daughter visited a month later, she noticed the mug and asked, 'Why haven't you thrown this away?'

Meera just said, 'Because it still holds warmth.'

Tara smiled. 'Like you.'

But let's pause here and turn to ourselves. Because Priya's story is ours too.

Life is far from perfect. We don't need a perfect body, a perfect job, a perfect house or a perfect partner for life to be joyous. And yet most of us spend so much energy chasing 'perfect' that we miss the simple, imperfect joys right in front of us. For example, have you ever tried to find the 'perfect' parking spot? You circle endlessly, frustrated, only to end up back at the first spot you rejected ten minutes ago. That's life in a nutshell—chasing perfection when 'good enough' would've worked beautifully!

And that's what Wabi-Sabi is about.[2] It is a philosophy that teaches us to see beauty in what is flawed, humble and unfinished—to celebrate imperfection, impermanence and incompleteness.

When I first heard the word 'Wabi-Sabi', I'll admit I thought it was either a new sushi roll or a distant cousin of wasabi. I imagined it might make my nose burn. Instead, it opened my eyes. Wabi-Sabi is a way of seeing the world. One that says life's cracks and asymmetries are not to be hidden or erased—they are to be embraced.

And isn't that thought liberating? That our worth isn't erased by our wrinkles, failures, losses or detours. That beauty doesn't live in perfection—it lives in authenticity.

Think of how it plays out in our personal lives, where perfection whispers every day that we must look a certain way—flawless skin, flat stomach, thick, shiny hair. Wabi-Sabi replies: 'The lines on your face are life's calligraphy. They're proof you've smiled, cried and lived.' And isn't that more beautiful than an airbrushed selfie?

In relationships, we imagine love will be like a perfectly scripted movie. But real love is full of bloopers—mismatched moods, unfinished sentences and forgotten anniversaries. Yet sometimes, it's these 'cracks' that make the bond real. The inside jokes, the scars you carry together, the fight that ends in laughter—these are not flaws, they're the gold that fills the space between two people.

In our work, perfection demands that every report be a work of art and every presentation a TED Talk. Wabi-Sabi reminds us that excellence doesn't mean flawlessness—it means sincerity. You will forget a pie chart. You will mispronounce a word. You may even send a message to the wrong group chat (and realize your new manager now knows what the office thinks of him). But these stumbles don't erase your value, they humanize it.

And then there's life itself—unpredictable, impermanent, unfinished. Friendships fade, hair greys, bodies change, people leave. If we wait for perfection to enjoy life, we'll keep waiting forever. Wabi-Sabi asks us to hold the chipped vase, place flowers in it and notice how they bloom despite the crack.

Which brings us back to Kintsugi. You've already seen it in Meera's story—the art of repairing broken pottery with gold, making the cracks the most beautiful part of the object. That's what Wabi-Sabi looks like in practice. Not giving up on ourselves when life marks us, but highlighting those very marks as proof of resilience.

And maybe that's what Priya needed to hear that night. That a crack doesn't disqualify you from beauty, self-worth or love. It can, if you let it, become the very place from where the light enters.

~

When I finished, Priya sat in silence for a long moment, her eyes still on the crack in her own coffee cup. She ran her finger lightly along the rim, tracing the fracture. Then she looked up at me, her eyes moist but steadier than before. 'Meera saw gold in her cracks,' she said gently. 'Maybe I can too.'

There was no dramatic shift, no instant transformation—just a little smile tugging at her lips. And sometimes, that is how healing begins: not with thunderclaps, but with the smallest, quietest nod to hope.

'But now tell me, Swamiji ...' she said with a mischievous grin, 'doesn't this whole Wabi-Sabi thing—this acceptance of imperfection—also risk becoming the perfect excuse for laziness? Imagine me telling my client: "Don't expect the report on time, I'm practising Wabi-Sabi!" Or telling my trainer: "Why run on the treadmill when my curves are Wabi-Sabi?"'

We broke into laughter. But beneath her joke lay a question as sharp as the crack on her cup: Does acceptance mean we stop striving to improve?

'Well, Priya, if Wabi-Sabi becomes the reason for missed deadlines and skipped workouts, then we'll have to open a whole new department—"Misapplied Japanese Philosophies".'

She chuckled.

'But I get what you mean,' I continued. 'Acceptance can sound like giving up. Yet true acceptance isn't apathy—it's the ground from which real growth begins. When we accept ourselves, we stop fighting who we are long enough to actually work on who we can become. Without that acceptance, improvement is driven by guilt, fear or comparison—and such improvement doesn't last.'

I gestured lightly towards her cup. 'Think of the crack. Wabi-Sabi doesn't say, "Leave it broken." It says, "Mend it with care. Highlight it. Learn from it." In the same way, acknowledging imperfection isn't about refusing to grow—it's about choosing to grow with compassion, not punishment. Progress, not perfection. Presence, not pressure.'

The lantern flickered between us. 'So no, Wabi-Sabi isn't an excuse to stop striving. It's the reason to strive more joyfully, more sustainably, because even during the process, we are already worthy.'

And that's when I decided to share with Priya a story I'd once read—the story of a corporate professional named Arjun. It's one we can all relate to, a gentle reminder of how to find balance between accepting what is and striving to become better.

∼

Arjun was forty when he decided to renovate his apartment. Not a full-blown demolition—just fresh paint, some decluttering, new curtains. Symbolic. A midlife restart.

He began with the bedroom wall opposite his bed. A calming olive green, earthy and grounding. He bought brushes, taped the edges of the wall to keep the borders clean, laid down drop cloths and painted diligently for two days.

Then life happened.

Work crises, ageing parents, weekend chaos. The wall remained half-painted—half olive, half faded-cream.

Weeks passed. Every night, Arjun stared at that two-tone wall and muttered to himself, 'Finish the damn wall.' But somehow, he didn't.

One Sunday, his friend Rhea visited. An artist at heart, she sipped her tea, glanced at the wall and smiled.

'Oh! I love this.'

'Love what?' Arjun groaned. 'My lazy unfinished wall?'

She laughed. 'No. The transition, the contrast, the rawness. It's honest. It's ... Wabi-Sabi.'

'Wabi-what?'

'Wabi-Sabi,' she explained, 'is the art of embracing imperfection. The reminder that life doesn't have to be flawless to be meaningful. It's not "don't finish the wall". It's "don't hate yourself if it takes time".'

That night, Arjun lay awake thinking. All his life he'd swung between extremes—all-in or all-out. Six days of hitting the gym at 6 a.m., then three weeks off because he missed one day. A month of salads and discipline, then a guilt-fuelled binge because he 'failed' by eating a snack.

Maybe he wasn't lazy. Maybe he was just ashamed of being unfinished. Of being in the middle.

The next morning, standing before the wall, he whispered, 'You're allowed to be halfway.'

He didn't pick up the paintbrush that day.

But he did go for a walk. He did cancel a pointless call. He did write two pages of the book he'd been postponing.

Not to avoid the wall, but because he stopped avoiding himself.

Over the next few weeks, he ate better. Not perfectly. Just better. He called his father. Not for long. But with presence. He kept promises. Not all of them. Just the ones that mattered.

And then one rainy Saturday afternoon, with chai placed on the windowsill and music in the room, he finally picked up the brush and painted the wall. Not to prove anything. Just to complete a conversation he had once started with himself.

Because Wabi-Sabi isn't about settling. It's about softening. It's not about staying flawed but about growing gently, from self-respect, not self-disgust.

When we stop demanding perfection,

We stop quitting so easily.

Because now, we're not failing—

We're simply continuing.

Like the wall.

Like life.

Like us.

~

I finished the story and let the words hang in the night air.

Priya hadn't touched her cup. She looked at me, her eyes searching. 'So Wabi-Sabi isn't about leaving the wall half-painted,' she said. 'It's about not hating yourself while you're still painting it.'

I nodded. 'Yes. Acceptance isn't opposed to growth—it's the space that allows growth to unfold.'

She leaned back, exhaling deeply, as though releasing something she had been carrying for years. 'Hmm,' she murmured, almost to herself. 'Maybe I've been mistaking unfinished for unworthy.'

In that moment, it wasn't about coffee mugs or half-painted walls any more. It was about Priya—and perhaps about all of us—learning that we are allowed to be works in progress and still be enough.

After a moment, Priya seemed ready to ask another question, but just then Ved appeared with Gaurav in tow.

'Mom!' He swooped in with a quick hug. 'Hope you're not boring Gaurji with your tragic backstories.'

Priya rolled her eyes with a grin. 'Excuse me, I was inspiring the monk—try that sometime.'

Ved chuckled and turned to me. 'So how's the evening been, Gaurji? I hope Mom's dose of inspiration hasn't scared you away yet.'

Before I could reply, Gaurav jumped in. 'If anyone's scaring people away, it's Ved. He's been running around like the unofficial MC of this wedding. I've counted at least three instances when he's repeated the same joke—and people still laughed, out of pity.'

Ved shot him a look. 'It's called brand consistency.'

I laughed, shaking my head. 'Well, you two seem to be enjoying yourselves.'

'Of course!' Ved said. 'We've had food, fun and roasted half our relatives—all in one evening. That's efficiency.'

Priya sighed dramatically. 'And this, Swamiji, is what I live with—Comedy Central, twenty-four-seven.'

We all laughed heartily. The mood, which just moments earlier had been heavy with reflection, was now buoyant again with humour and warmth.

As the evening stretched into night, I decided it was wise to retire. Not because the conversations weren't good—they were wonderful. But because even monks know when to quietly exit before someone ropes them into dancing to Bollywood remixes at midnight.

And so, I slipped away—leaving behind the music, the laughter and the buffet line that still looked longer than those seen in some pilgrimages. As I made my way to my room under the desert moonlight, my thoughts circled back to what had stayed with me that evening—the quiet wisdom of Kintsugi and Wabi-Sabi.

The cracks we carry can be repaired meaningfully. The imperfections we try to hide often hold their own kind of beauty. Life doesn't ask us to be flawless—it asks us to be authentic, to let our scars become strengths and our incompleteness become possibilities. That, perhaps, is the gentlest truth I carried with me into the night.

....

THINGS TO THINK ABOUT ...

HOLDING SPACE FOR GRIEF: When someone shares their pain, they don't need us to quickly 'make it better'. They need us to patiently 'let it be'. Often, it's the silence of compassion—not the noise of advice—that brings true healing.

THE GOLD IN THE CRACKS: Kintsugi—the Japanese art of repairing broken pottery with gold—reminds us that our scars and setbacks make us more beautiful when embraced with love and care.

THE BEAUTY OF WABI-SABI: We spend so much energy chasing perfection that we miss the simple, imperfect joys that are right in front of us. Wabi-Sabi is an outlook that celebrates imperfection, impermanence and incompleteness—beauty in what is humble, flawed and unfinished.

ACCEPTANCE WITH ASPIRATION: Wabi-Sabi doesn't mean giving up on growth in the name of acceptance. It's not escapism. It means holding both truths: Embracing life as it is, while still striving gently to improve. Acceptance gives us peace, aspiration gives us direction.

•••••••••••••••

The exercises related to the concepts mentioned in this chapter can be found on p. 264.

4

THE WISDOM OF THE LOTUS

How to Move from Lack to Fulfilment

~

Not all battles are won by force—some are won by the refusal to let bitterness command the soul.

I had just finished my morning sadhana—chanting, prayer and a few minutes of stillness, which always felt like punctuation marks adding nuance to the long sentence of life—and stepped out to bask in the silence of the morning.

The palace lawns at dawn felt like a different world from the night before. The same place that had throbbed with songs, dance and laughter just hours earlier was now washed in soft gold by the rising sun.

There's something magical about silence. It isn't just the absence of sound, it's the presence of something deeper. When we sit in silence, it's like looking into a mirror turned inward. We begin to see corners of our own hearts and minds that we didn't know existed. At first, it can be uncomfortable—because in silence there are no filters, no makeup, no patching up, no performance for anyone else. It is just us, as we are.

But it is in these precious, unfiltered moments that true reflection begins. Silence gives us the courage to face what we often avoid—the fear tucked beneath our confidence, the fatigue hidden behind our busyness, the longing beneath our laughter. And it also opens the door to something greater—a connection with our own inner self.

Our mind is like a battlefield of thoughts. Desires clash with doubts, fears wrestle with hopes, expectations collide with reality, ego locks swords with humility. In the constant noise of responsibilities, deadlines and social pressures, we often don't hear the battle inside. But in silence, the battlefield comes into view. And that is the first step to peace—not because the battle has ended, but because we stop identifying with every sword that swings. We become the witness, not just the warrior.

Spiritual practices like chanting, meditation or prayer can help us enter that silence more deeply, but sometimes simply walking in a quiet garden at dawn can be a spiritual act. Silence has its own language, if we dare to listen. And that is why our sadhana becomes the gentle rhythm of our day—a constant that keeps us anchored amidst all the change.

It was in that stillness, with the morning dew sparkling on the grass and the desert breeze brushing gently against my face, that I noticed I wasn't alone.

Across the lawn, walking slowly with a steaming cup of chai in his hand, was Gaurav—Sanjana's elder brother—whom I had briefly met the night before. He was dressed in understated casuals: a plain-grey T-shirt, navy track pants and running shoes. His hair was slightly tousled, as though he had just rolled out of bed, and his stride was unhurried, each step carrying the weight of his thoughts. When he looked up and noticed me, his smile was both warm and a little weary, like that of someone who had been up late not just celebrating but also reflecting.

'Swamiji! Early riser, huh?' he called out, lifting his cup in greeting. 'No hangover from last night's dance floor?'

I chuckled. 'A monk's best move on the dance floor is the exit. I escaped before anyone could pull me in.'

Gaurav laughed. 'Smart! I wasn't so lucky. I was dragged into some choreographed number. Half the time I was trying to remember the steps, and the rest of the time I was trying not to trip.'

We fell into step together, the gravel crunching softly beneath us. For a while, we simply walked in companionable silence, listening to the calls of the birds flitting across the morning sky.

Then Gaurav tilted his head slightly, as though weighing a thought, and gave me a sidelong glance. 'You know, I've actually seen a few of your videos online.'

I raised an eyebrow. 'And you still chose to walk beside me? Brave man.'

That drew a proper laugh from him. 'No, really. One clip stuck with me—you spoke about how life sometimes pushes us into roles we never asked for, but that playing them with love makes us stronger. That one ... felt like you were talking to me.'

I smiled. 'Thank you for sharing that. You know, I often send these words out into the world like paper boats, not knowing if they'll sink or sail. Hearing that one of them reached you safely, that's my reward.'

Gaurav nodded slowly, swirling the chai in his cup. 'Paper boats, huh? I like that. Some sink, some float ... some get lost, some reach the shore.'

'And sometimes they land in places we never expected—like this conversation on a palace lawn after a late-night dance party.'

He chuckled. 'Yeah, life has a way of surprising us like that. You put something out there, never knowing who'll catch it.'

For a few seconds, he stayed quiet, as though mulling over whether to continue or not. 'The funny thing is,' he murmured, 'most people think of weddings as loud, bright, over the top. But mornings like these ... they make you remember what's beneath all that razzle-dazzle.'

I nodded. 'Silence reveals what the noise hides.'

Gaurav exhaled, his breath visible in the morning chill. Then, for a moment, his gaze drifted past the lawns towards some place much further away.

'See, my parents died in a car accident when I was twenty-one,' he began, his words slower, more deliberate now. 'Sanjana was only thirteen then. Overnight, I stopped being just her elder brother. I became parent, guardian, alarm clock, ATM, tuition teacher … everything.' He gave a wry smile. 'Relatives swooped in and took what little we had. Only the house stayed with us. I was still pursuing my commerce degree, but I took up whatever jobs I could find to keep the house running. While my friends were partying, I was paying bills and fees.'

We continued to walk. A squirrel darted across the path just then, pausing for a moment with something clasped tightly in its mouth before scurrying up a tree. Gaurav's gaze followed it briefly, and he gave a slight, ironic smile.

'That's how it's been for me,' he said. 'Always carrying something in my mouth, in my hands, on my back … Never free to just be. And since my parents left this world, I never really thought of marriage or my own life. Sanjana became my life. She's the reason I worked, sacrificed and stayed strong. So yeah, when you said in that video that the responsibility you never chose can become the very thing that shapes you, it … hit home.'

He walked a few more steps in silence, then added, almost as if he wanted to balance his admission with something lighter, 'Look, I'm deeply grateful I could be there for Sanjana. If I had to do it all over again, I would. Not once have I allowed myself to complain about it, not once have I shown resentment. Ask anyone, and they'll tell you that I'm the one who's always cracking jokes, lightening the mood, being helpful. And that's all true.'

When he spoke again, his voice had become quieter. 'But you know ... somewhere, in a corner of my heart, there's a bitterness that lingers. A taste I can't wash away. Life feels unjust sometimes. Parents taken so early, our childhood stolen overnight. Everyone remembers me as the smiling one, the strong one. But in the dark hours, when Sanjana was asleep and I was alone with my thoughts, I wanted to ask: Why us? Why her at thirteen? Why me at twenty-one? Why do some kids get to remain kids while others are forced into adulthood before they're ready?'

He tightened his grip on the chai cup. 'I never let Sanjana feel it, of course. She only saw a brother who was steady, never shaken. But inside ... I've carried that bitterness. Not enough to turn me hard, I suppose, but enough to make me wonder what life might have been like if it hadn't been so cruel at the start ...'

He glanced sideways at me, his eyes tired but searching, as though waiting for something—not answers, but understanding.

The desert breeze filled the silence between us, carrying the weight of his words more eloquently than I ever could. I simply nodded, slowly, deliberately, letting him know I had heard him, really heard him.

Then I gently said, 'Sometimes, life drafts us into battles we never volunteered for. But the way you've stood your ground—Sanjana's not just lucky, she's blessed.'

I let that rest a moment before continuing. 'Gaurav, strength is often misunderstood. People think it means you feel no bitterness, no doubt, no grief. But real strength isn't the absence of those things. It's the discipline of not letting them win. You may have carried your bitterness, yes—and that's absolutely natural and human for someone who has gone through what you have—but you never let it make you bitter. You never let it lessen your love or stop you from being Sanjana's shelter from the downpour of challenging times. And you never let it take away your smile, your laughter, your humour. That's not weakness. That's victory.'

Gaurav's shoulders eased, as though the burden he'd been bearing had lightened. His eyes drifted towards the horizon where the sunlight was creeping across the lawns. A grateful smile grew on his lips.

∼

If there is one constant in life, dear reader, it is that life is full of challenges and disappointments. Things we never wanted end up coming our way. Things we never thought could happen actually happen. Our carefully built hopes may get crushed, our well-laid plans may be foiled and our brightest dreams may sometimes shatter right before our eyes. And when that happens, life has a way of making us bitter—often silently, almost invisibly, on the inside.

Bitterness doesn't always look like anger or loud complaints. Sometimes it hides behind humour, behind busyness, behind that well-rehearsed smile we wear for the world. But inside, there is a quiet voice whispering: Life has been unfair. Why me?

It could be something small—like spending weeks preparing for an exam, only to fall sick on the day you are supposed to take it. Or finally booking that dream holiday it took you years to save up for, only to have an emergency stop you from going at the last minute. It could be something bigger too—like pouring your heart into a relationship and then watching it fall apart without any explanation. Or working hard at your job, waiting patiently for recognition, only to be overlooked for a promotion.

And sometimes, it's not just about what we don't get but also about what we lose. A parent who leaves too early. A friend who drifts away. An opportunity that slips out of your reach. The pain of these moments is real, and no amount of positive thinking can instantly erase it.

When disappointment knocks on your door again and again, the danger is that we begin to build walls. We harden our hearts so we won't feel hurt again. We wear bitterness like an armour, thinking it will protect us. But bitterness doesn't protect us, it poisons us. It keeps us alive on the outside but drains us on the inside.

Yet—and this is where hope enters—every bitter experience also carries within it the seed of something better. The question is not whether life will give us wounds, there is no doubt that it will. The question is will those wounds harden us or will they make us wiser, gentler and more compassionate?

Gaurav's story is proof of this. He carried the bitterness of loss, yes, but he never let it calcify into resentment. Instead, he channelled that pain into responsibility, love and humour. He did not allow tragedy to mould him into hardness. Instead, he rewrote it into strength.

And that is the lesson. Life will keep giving us things we never asked for—extra responsibilities, sudden illnesses, financial strains, heartbreaks. We may not be able to control what comes our way, but we can still choose how we receive it. Bitterness shrinks us. Responsibility, faith and love expand us. Pain will come either way, but whether it becomes poison or power depends on how we hold it.

I remember two dear friends of mine—both much older than me, yet somehow we connected deeply. Sadly, both are no more. One passed away during the Covid pandemic and the other while on a holiday. I miss them even today, and their wise words still echo in my mind. Interestingly, both had completely opposite takes on life.

One used to say: 'Life is unfair. Get used to it.' The other would insist: 'Life is unfair. Learn to negotiate.'

Now, who was right and who was wrong? The truth is neither was wrong. Both were right.

There are things in life that are completely beyond our control. The death of a loved one. An accident. A sudden illness. What negotiation can we do in such situations? None. In those moments, acceptance is the only way forward. Life is unfair—get used to it.

But there are also many situations where we can act, where our choices and efforts make a difference. Like Gaurav taking responsibility for his and Sanjana's lives. Like working through financial setbacks, strained relationships or professional challenges. Here, life may still be unfair, but we can negotiate, adapt and turn things around. Life is unfair—learn to negotiate.

Think about it in an everyday context. At work, your boss may make a decision you don't agree with. Some parts of it may be non-negotiable; you simply have to accept them. But other parts you can influence through dialogue, performance and persistence. In marriage, there will be personality traits in your spouse you cannot change—that's acceptance. But household responsibilities can be shared. That's negotiation. In terms of our health, we cannot stop ageing—that's acceptance. But we can eat wisely, exercise and care for our bodies—that's negotiation.

Maturity and wisdom lie in knowing the difference between when to accept things and when to negotiate. Accepting what cannot be changed brings peace. Negotiating what can be changed brings growth. And somewhere between the two lies our resilience.

As I thought of this, I glanced at Gaurav walking beside me. He had accepted the tragedy of losing his parents, something no amount of struggle could undo. And yet, in the same breath, he had negotiated with life—taking on responsibilities, fighting setbacks, making sure Sanjana had a future. His story carried both truths: acceptance and negotiation.

And perhaps that is the choice life places before each of us, every day—to stay bitter or to grow better. To be hardened by pain or deepened by it. To say, 'Life is unfair, but I must endure,' as well as, 'Life is unfair, but I will engage.'

That is how bitterness turns into wisdom. That is how wounds turn into resilience. And that is how ordinary struggles turn us into extraordinary people.

However, in light of everything we have discussed above, we must remember to be very careful. This approach should not slip into toxic positivity—the kind that dismisses pain, trivializes struggle or offers false hope in the name of cheerfulness. To say 'accept pain' must never mean we become insensitive, either to our own suffering or to that of others.

The truth is that not everyone has the same capacity to cope. Some rise quickly from adversity, drawing strength from their inner reserves or from the support systems around them. Others may take months, even years, to find their footing. And there are those who, for a season or sometimes longer, simply want to stay with their pain—not to wallow, but because their heart is not yet ready to move on. That, too, is valid.

Betterment, then, is not a destination to be reached immediately, nor a race where the fastest are the strongest. It is a journey. Sometimes slow. Sometimes uneven. Sometimes two steps forward and one step back. What matters is not how quickly we move, but that we keep moving.

Equally important is how we treat ourselves along the way. If we pressure ourselves to 'be better' instantly, we add guilt on top of grief. If we force ourselves to smile when our soul is breaking, we deepen the crack. Compassion begins with letting ourselves be human—to cry without shame, to pause without guilt and to rise again only when our spirit is ready.

The balance is this: to honour the reality of pain, yet not let pain become our only reality. To feel it fully but not be consumed by it. To accept both joy and sorrow as teachers—each shaping us in ways the other cannot.

∼

As Gaurav and I walked, our conversation weaving between silence and the sharing of thoughts, we found ourselves by a pond. The morning breeze sent lazy ripples across the water where lotus flowers floated, their petals slowly opening to the sun. We paused and, without a word, sat down on a stone bench nearby.

'Swamiji,' he said at last, 'I've tried so many things. A couple of ventures too. I was sincere, hardworking, smart, or at least I thought I was. But every time ... I was met with failure. Sometimes it was my fault, sometimes because of betrayal. Family cheated us, and later even business partners I trusted turned against me.'

He shook his head, still staring at the pond. 'And then I look at people like the Aroras—so successful, so well-off. How does one make sense of it? There are so many sincere people out there, giving their 200 per cent, pouring their hearts into what they do. Yet the outcomes are so different. Some soar, some stumble. Some win, some keep losing. And I am not asking this question out of envy but out of honesty. Why, Swamiji, is life so unfair?'

I watched the lotus flowers swaying gently on the water's surface. 'Gaurav,' I said, 'do you see these lotuses? They don't rise away from the mud—they rise because of it. The same mud that looks messy gives them the strength to bloom.

'Life works in a similar way,' I continued. 'Some find themselves in clean ponds, some in swampy waters. We can't control that part. To some it looks like destiny, to others karma, to some just coincidence. Philosophers may debate it endlessly, but in the end, none of us chose our starting point. What matters is not the pond we inherit, but the flower we allow ourselves to become.'

I paused. 'Effort is important, Gaurav—but the outcome is not always in our hands. We see hardworking, sincere people struggle, while others who cut corners seem to succeed. It feels unfair. And maybe, in a worldly sense, it is. But life is not a balance sheet of effort versus reward. It's a classroom. Every person is taught lessons suited to their journey. Some lessons teach you about abundance, some about loss. Some about applause, some about betrayal.

'The question is not: Is life unfair? But rather: What am I meant to learn from what life has given me? Because the pond may differ, but the invitation is the same—to rise, to grow, to blossom.'

I looked at the pond. 'And remember, even if a lotus rises slowly, even if it blossoms late, it still fulfils its purpose. Its value is not diminished by when or where it blooms. Besides, Gaurav ... lotuses don't sit around comparing bloom times on LinkedIn. They just rise when it's their season.'

Gaurav chuckled. 'True, Swamiji. Though if lotuses *did* have LinkedIn accounts, I'm sure the Aroras would still be posting motivational quotes about "blooming early".'

I laughed with him, grateful for the humour softening the heaviness of his burden.

∽

Dear friends, the example of the lotus reminds us of a simple truth: Focus on what we can change, rather than losing ourselves in what we can't. And to explain that, let's look at the life of a farmer.

Now, tell me—what's the most important thing for a good harvest? Most of you will say, 'The land, of course!' And you're right. If the soil is barren, even the farmer's best efforts may not yield much.

But fertile land alone doesn't guarantee success. The farmer also needs skill. He must know when to plough, how to sow, when to water and when to wait. A good farmer can draw life even from average soil. An unskilled farmer, on the other hand, can waste even the most fertile land simply by not knowing what to do with it.

And then come the resources. Good seeds, irrigation, fertilizers. Without these, even the best farmer can only hope.

Now, picture this—fertile land, skilled farmer, good resources. Sounds perfect, doesn't it? But if the farmer spends all his time sleeping under a tree, watching the clouds go by, even the best land won't yield crops. Effort matters. As the saying goes, 'Hard work beats talent when talent doesn't work hard.'

But there's a twist. Even when the farmer has it all—land, skill, resources and effort—there is one thing completely out of his hands: the rains. Without them, nothing grows.

So here's the wisdom that the Gita offers:

karmaṇy evādhikāras te
mā phaleṣu kadācana
mā karma-phala-hetur bhūr
mā te saṅgo 'stv akarmaṇi

You have the right to perform your actions,
but not to the fruits of those actions.
Let not the results be your motive,
nor let your attachment be to inaction. (2.47)

So focus on the things that you can control. And bow humbly before the ones you cannot. Don't punish yourself when things don't go your way. And don't get too proud when they do. Both the farmer and the rains play their part.

And isn't life just like this? We do everything right—study hard, show up at work, give our best in relationships. And still, sometimes, the outcome isn't what we hoped for. We start wondering, What's wrong with me? But maybe nothing's wrong with us. Maybe it just didn't rain.

Now, of course, it's natural to feel hurt or frustrated when that happens. We're human. But the wisdom of the Gita reminds us: Don't stay stuck there. Don't live your whole life chasing the clouds. Instead, keep ploughing, sowing and giving your best. It will rain when it's meant to.

Take Dhritarashtra from the Mahabharata. He was blind from birth, and he made that his entire identity. He lived his whole life trapped in the I-don't-have-this mindset, clinging to a throne that wasn't rightfully his. Yet the scriptures also say he had immense physical strength—a gift he could have used in countless meaningful ways. But he didn't. He wasted his life comparing and complaining instead of cultivating what he did have.

And that's the secret, my friends. Stop chasing what's missing. Start with what's in your hands. Work with it. Build on it. Because the truth is, none of us can control the rain—

but each of us can still prepare the soil, plant the seeds and tend to the field.

So let's not use karma or destiny as excuses. We may never fully know why something happened to us, but the question isn't: 'Why me?' The real question is: 'What now?'

There's a simple saying: If you're bitten by a snake, and instead of treating the poison you waste your time chasing the snake, you'll lose your life. In the same way, if we spend all our energy chasing explanations, we miss the healing.

I'm reminded of a tongue-twister we all struggled with in school: 'Betty bought a bit of butter, but the bit of butter was too bitter. So Betty bought a bit of better butter to make the bitter butter better.'

Try saying that quickly—it's fun! But behind the laughter lies a life lesson. When we're handed a bit of bitter butter—disappointments, betrayals, setbacks—we can either complain, feel defeated and stay bitter. Or we can be like Betty and look for better butter: a better attitude, a better effort, a better version of ourselves that can turn bitterness into growth.

And one scoop of that better butter is taking responsibility for our lives with wisdom. Sometimes that wisdom comes from two lenses—like my friends once told me: 'Life is unfair, get used to it' and 'Life is unfair, learn to negotiate.' Sometimes it comes from nature—like the lotus rising out of the mud or the farmer who works his land while still bowing to the rain.

The balance of accepting what is beyond our control and changing what is in our control, of being grateful for what we have while striving for what we don't, that is what transforms life's bitter butter into something a little more bearable, and sometimes even better.

~

Gaurav broke the silence. 'Swamiji, you've given me a lot to think about. Maybe … maybe it's time I stop staring at the water … and start rowing my boat.'

I nodded. 'That's a wise thought. And remember, Gaurav, you don't have to row alone.'

'What do you mean?'

I smiled. 'Let me tell you about the cigarette lighter that I pulled out during a talk once.'

Gaurav raised his eyebrows. 'A monk … with a lighter?'

I laughed. 'The audience had the same reaction! They were half shocked, half amused. Anyway, I lit the lighter so everyone could see the flame. Then I put it into a glass and started pouring water over it—bit by bit, until the lighter was completely submerged in water. Then I pulled it back out and tried flicking it again. Nothing. It just wouldn't light.

'And I told the gathering—that's what life often does to us. It drowns our spark. Disappointments, failures, betrayals, stress. One wave after another until the will to grow, to love, to live, feels extinguished.'

Gaurav nodded quietly.

I went on. 'But then I pulled out another lighter.'

Gaurav chuckled. 'Two lighters? You really are full of surprises, Swamiji.'

I grinned. 'Yes, the audience thought so too. I said—this lighter can't light itself again. But this other one can. And then I used the second flame to bring back the first. That's the power of support. We can't always fight our battles alone. Sometimes we need someone else to reignite our spark when we can't find it ourselves.'

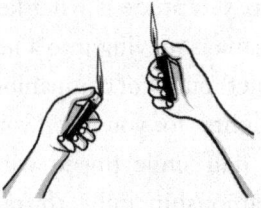

I paused, then added gently, 'Isn't that what you and Sanjana have done for each other? You supported her when she was young and fragile. And in her own way, she's supported you too. That's why, despite everything, both of you haven't allowed bitterness to completely take over. You've kept each other's flame alive.'

Gaurav sighed. 'You know, Swamiji ... I never thought of it like that. But yes ... maybe we really have been each other's lighters.'

I nodded. 'Support, Gaurav—that's what keeps us going. Sometimes it comes from family, sometimes from friends and sometimes from the invisible hands of well-wishers we may never fully know. And for many, it's also that deeper spiritual connection—with the universe, with God—that allows us to tap into a power beyond what this material world can offer.

'That's why no one should ever feel like they have to fight alone. We are carried more than we realize—by love, friendship and grace. And it is that support which turns bitterness into the courage to keep moving forward.'

Gaurav was quiet for a while. Then he said softly, almost as if he was confessing, 'I guess ... I owe more to Sanjana—and to the people who've stood by me—than I've ever admitted to myself. I've always been so busy holding the lighter for her that I forgot I might need one too.'

I placed a hand lightly on his shoulder. 'Acknowledging that is the first step. Gratitude is what keeps the spark alive. And now that Sanjana is moving into a new phase of her life, perhaps it's time you thought of companionship too. Someone who can hold the lighter for you when your hands are tired.'

Gaurav gave a half-smile tinged with both wistfulness and mirth. 'Companionship, huh? You're making me sound like an old lantern in need of a caretaker.'

I chuckled. 'Not a caretaker, Gaurav—a companion. Someone to share the journey with, to remind you that even strong men need soft places to rest.'

Gaurav looked away for a moment, the playfulness in his eyes giving way to something gentler, more contemplative. 'Maybe you're right, Swamiji ... maybe it's time I stop thinking of myself only as Sanjana's shelter and allow myself to find one too.'

Our conversation brought to mind some lines that have stayed with me for years:

Chhote se dil mein gam bahut hai,
Zindagi ne diye zakhm bahut hai,
Kab ki maar daalti ye zaalim duniya humein,
Kambakht in doston ki duaaon mein dum bahut hai.

This small heart holds a lot of sorrow,
life has given me too many wounds.
The world would have finished me off long ago—
If not for the strength hidden in the good wishes of my friends.

And isn't that the truth? Life may hand us the pain, betrayals or burdens we never asked for—but the presence of those who care for us, pray for us and stand quietly behind us can transform the texture of that pain for the better.

So yes, a bitter life becomes a better life with such people, prayers and shoulders. Responsibility gives us direction, support gives us strength. One without the other is a lonely road. Together they make the journey not just bearable but meaningful.

By the time we stepped into the palace, the quiet of the lawns was replaced by a different kind of rhythm. The dining hall was buzzing now. Guests were trickling in, waiters balancing trays of parathas and kettles of chai were moving between the tables. Conversations floated through the air, mixing with the clatter of plates. And there, at a table by the window, was a lady whose laughter rose above it all—brighter and louder than the rest of the room.

'Gaurav *beta!* Swamiji!' She waved to us dramatically, her bangles jingling. 'Here, here! Don't sit anywhere else. Sit with me—my poor breakfast was getting bored all alone!'

It was Rukmini Dadi, Rakesh's mother. I had heard about her, but this was our first meeting. She was exactly as people had described. There was an unmistakable twinkle in her eyes. She was the kind of person who bravely faces all of life's struggles and still chooses to laugh in the rain.

As we sat down, she leaned forward conspiratorially and said, 'I was resting yesterday after that long journey. These knees of mine, they protest like trade unions. But today? Full energy! Now, Swamiji, tell me one thing honestly—what do monks even eat for breakfast? Or do you just live on air and blessings?'

Gaurav grinned. 'Dadi, Swamiji eats like the rest of us—he just skips the gossip part.'

She smacked Gaurav's arm playfully. 'Arré, gossip is nutrition, beta! Don't underestimate it. It keeps the mind sharp and the tongue sharper.'

We laughed as the waiter brought over a basket of aloo parathas glistening with ghee. Dadi tore into one with the enthusiasm of someone twenty years younger. 'Doctors say no ghee. I say what's the point of living long if you can't live well? Better to live a happy and short life than a grumpy and long one!'

I smiled. 'That's wisdom, Dadi. Except I suspect you're going to live both long and happy—just to prove the doctors wrong.'

Her eyes sparkled. 'Exactly, Swamiji! And let me tell you—don't ever believe anyone who says Punjabis can't diet. We can. It's just that our diet begins after the parathas are over.'

Gaurav shook his head, laughing. 'Dadi, you haven't changed one bit.'

She smiled. 'You know, life tested me early. I lost my husband when Rakesh was just a boy. People whispered, "How will she manage?" But I told myself: If the world doubts me, I'll prove them wrong by laughing louder. And see, here we are today. My son has done well, my grandchildren are flying, and I still enjoy my parathas. Why cry when you can keep the fire going?'

Her words carried the weight of truth, wrapped in humour. And in that moment, I realized something. Gaurav embodied sacrifice, Priya carried scars, but Rukmini Dadi was all sunshine. Together, they painted the picture of a family that was not perfect but human. It was proof that strength can wear many faces: silent, scarred or smiling.

As we finished, Dadi patted my hand warmly. 'Swamiji, stay close for the next three days. I'll be better company than all these serious people here. Gaurav is sweet but too sensible. Priya is lovely but too quiet. Ved is funny but too phone-obsessed. And me? I am the full package—wisdom, jokes and a bit of masala. Balance is important, no?'

I folded my hands with a laugh. 'Then Dadi, I think you've just become my favourite breakfast companion.'

We laughed so much that morning the waiters kept refilling our chai just to linger near the joy. And as I watched her, I was reminded of my own grandmother, whom I called Dadi too.

She lived to a hundred, and in that century of her life she experienced more than what most hearts could endure. She lost her husband. She lost her son. She lost two daughters and three grandsons. Yet, through all of this, she held the family together, always with a smile on her face.

After my father's passing, once the rituals were done, I had to leave. I was worried about my mother and Dadi, two elderly ladies at home alone. But Dadi didn't stop me. She assured me, calmly, that she would take care of everything, and that I was just a phone call away. There was no fear in her—only courage.

At ninety-two, when she was diagnosed with cancer, she faced chemo. In the hospital, she fell and broke her spine. Surgery, physiotherapy, and then, unbelievably, she was back on her feet, not dependent on anyone. At ninety-six, she fell again, another fracture, another surgery, more recovery—and again she walked.

During Covid, she fell yet again. With the lockdown looming, my mother and sister had to make the heartbreaking decision to move her to a care home. When my mother broke down and told her of the plan, Dadi smiled through her pain and simply said, 'It's fine. I'll manage.' And she did.

Even at ninety-nine, after another fall, she recovered enough to walk with a walker. When I visited her after the first wave of the pandemic, she was serene—no complaints, no bitterness. Just grace. Two weeks later, at the age of a hundred, she left the world ... but not our hearts.

She raised me with deep affection, and when I performed her last rites, what I carried most was her spirit which refused to become bitter. 'Life will make me cry,' she seemed to say, 'but I will still choose to smile.'

Sitting with Rukmini Dadi now, I realized that women like her embody an iron will. No wonder the first two letters of the word 'female' are 'fe' the symbol of iron. My mother and sister are the same. Of course, strength has nothing to do with gender—it is a matter of choice, of resilience, of refusing to surrender when the winds turn harsh. But when I think of my dadi, I am reminded of how extraordinary it is to choose to smile when life has given you every reason to weep.

As children, one of the things we most looked forward to the most during festivals were the fireworks. And our favourite? The sparklers. When lit, they burst into thousands of tiny sparks—each lasting only a few seconds, yet creating a dazzling effect together.

The small joys in life are like those sparks. A joke at breakfast, the taste of a hot paratha, the warmth of a kind word—these may seem fleeting, but together they create the glow that gives us strength. And it is this glow, gathered over days and years, that helps us endure the darker nights and heavier days that inevitably come our way.

So how do we keep that smile in the middle of chaos? How do we hold our light when the winds of life threaten to snuff it out? There are two simple but powerful practices to keep in mind:

- **Acceptance:** The courage to stop resisting what cannot be changed, and in that stillness, to find peace.
- **Faith:** The conviction that pain may test us, but it cannot break our spirit unless we let it.

That's what kept Dadi strong and smiling. And that's the third scoop of better butter that makes life better—the quiet glow of small joys, fuelled by acceptance and sustained by faith.

∽

As we rose from the table, still chuckling over Dadi's last quip, a sudden clatter rang out near the service counter. One of the young butlers had dropped a tray of glasses, and in his attempt to pick them up quickly, he had nicked his palm on the shards.

The boy froze, embarrassed, clutching his hand to hide the blood. Most guests glanced at the spectacle and then turned right back to their food. But before I could even stand up, Gaurav was already at the scene.

'Careful, bro,' he said gently, crouching down to steady the boy. 'It'll be okay. We're here.' He took the boy's hand, checked the cut and, with calm assurance, asked another staff member for a first-aid kit. He pressed a clean napkin around the wound, speaking in the kind of tone that heals wounds faster than medicine. 'You'll be all right. It's just a small cut. Don't worry.'

At that moment, Priya and Ved walked in. Priya paused, her eyes softening at Gaurav's tenderness. Ved, of course, broke the silence with a quip.

'Gaurav Uncle!' Ved exclaimed dramatically. 'Forget weddings—you're ready to open your own hospital!'

Gaurav laughed, still focused on tying the bandage. 'No, just doing what anyone should do when someone's hurt.'

Priya, still watching him, said, 'But not everyone would.'

The butler, still embarrassed but visibly calmer, whispered a grateful 'thank you' before slipping back to his duties. Gaurav brushed it off with a smile, returning to us as if nothing had happened.

But something had happened. A small act of care had revealed a big truth—that service is not always about grand gestures. Often, it is about the quick reflex to ease someone's pain, the instinct to be present when it matters most. When pain hardens us, service softens us.

Bitterness thrives in self-absorption, when our mind loops endlessly around *my hurt, my failure, my loss*. But the moment we look outwards, the cycle breaks. Helping someone else—even in a small way—reminds us that we are not defined only by what we lack but also by what we give.

Think about the times you've gone out of your way to comfort a friend, to cheer up a child, to help a colleague—wasn't there a strange feeling of lightness afterwards? Service doesn't erase our scars—it gives them meaning. It turns pain into purpose.

This reminded me of Dashrath Manjhi, the 'Mountain Man' from Bihar. His inspiring life story has been documented by multiple Indian news outlets,[1] and in the film *Manjhi: The Mountain Man* (2015). Dashrath's wife died because she couldn't get timely medical help after being injured; the closest hospital was on the other side of a mountain that blocked the way. Grief could have made him bitter for life. Instead, with nothing but a hammer and chisel, he began carving a road through that mountain. For twenty-two years he worked alone, until the 110-metre road was complete—reducing the distance between his village and the nearest medical centre from 55 kilometres to just 15.

A personal tragedy became his mission to help others. A wound became a pathway for others to be helped. His story reminds us that when life cuts us deeply, we can let the wound make us bitter or we can let it carve out something better for us.

Few of us will move mountains with simple tools as Dashrath Manjhi did. But in our own way, each of us can transform our struggles into strength. We can choose to use our pain to add value to someone else's life. And when we do, we will find that service not only heals others, it softens our own bitterness too.

As Gaurav sat back down with us, Priya's gaze lingered on him. Something in her eyes had shifted. She wasn't just looking at a man who had helped a butler with a cut on his palm—she was seeing someone kind, sensitive and deeply caring, someone who instinctively reached out to ease another's hurt. Quiet strength often speaks louder than words, and in that moment, Gaurav's actions meant more than any speech ever could.

• • • • • • • • • • • • • • • •

THINGS TO THINK ABOUT ...

THE MIRROR OF SILENCE: Silence isn't empty—it's a doorway to the self. In stillness, our hidden fears and longings surface, teaching us to witness them with calm instead of battling them in haste.

LIFE'S UNFAIRNESS—THE TWO LENSES: 'Get used to it' and 'Learn to negotiate' are both true. Wisdom is knowing when to accept and when to act.

BALANCING POSITIVITY WITH REALITY: We need to acknowledge pain for what it is, but not let it define us. To feel it deeply, yet not drown in it. To welcome both joy and sorrow as companions on our journey—each teaching us something the other never could.

LESSONS FROM THE LOTUS: We don't choose the mud or the pond, but we can choose to rise and bloom—late or early, clear water or murky.

THE GITA FRAMEWORK: Stop searching for what isn't there; begin with what is. Work with what you already have and let it grow. The truth is, none of us can command the rain—but we can still plough the soil, plant the seeds and prepare for the harvest. Karma and destiny aren't excuses to stay still, they're reminders to act wisely. We may never fully understand why something happens, but the question isn't 'Why me?', it's 'What can I do now?'

RISING ABOVE BITTERNESS:
- When life serves us a taste of bitterness—disappointments, betrayals or setbacks—we can either stay resentful or look for what can make us better, not bitter.
- And what is this better butter made of? Four scoops that sweeten life's harshness:
  1. **Responsibility:** Choosing wisdom over victimhood.
  2. **Support:** Leaning on the lighters around us, the people who rekindle our spark.
  3. **Small Joys:** Those sparkler-like moments that brighten even the darkest nights.
  4. **Service:** Softening our pain by easing another's.

STRENGTH WITH A SMILE: Even when the challenges of life threaten to extinguish our light, two quiet practices help us keep it alive:
- **Acceptance:** The strength to stop fighting what cannot be changed, and in that surrender, to discover calm.
- **Faith:** The trust that pain can shake us, but it cannot pull us down unless we let it.

•••••••••••••••

The exercises related to the concepts mentioned in this chapter can be found on p. 266.

5

THE MEHENDI MOSAIC

Giving Colour to Unspoken Dreams

~

Duty makes us reliable, dreams make us alive.
A meaningful life is built when we learn to
carry both.

The air buzzed with excitement. Women gathered in clusters, their hands and feet extended towards the mehendi artists, who bent over with steady focus, tracing delicate paisleys and peacocks with their henna cones. Children squealed with delight as their palms were decorated with simple designs, running off impatiently before the paste had dried. Laughter, dholak beats and the clinking of bangles filled the air.

For Sanjana, seated in the centre with her friends, the moment was surreal. Her hands, heavy with intricate designs, felt like canvases of love and tradition. Lakshmi flitted about, making sure everyone had their snacks and drinks, while Priya's eyes became tender at the sight of Ved. He was sitting slightly away from the crowd, doodling in a sketchbook with quiet concentration. She admired the way he saw beauty in the details that others missed.

Amid the festive laughter, someone leaned towards me and asked with a half-smile, 'Swamiji, why is this mehendi ceremony even part of a wedding? Isn't it just an excuse for more dancing, food and fun?'

I chuckled. 'Well, there's joy in that too, and joy itself is sacred. But mehendi isn't just about decoration. It has a deep symbolism. It is said to bring good fortune, love and prosperity to the couple. And they say the darker the colour of the mehendi, the deeper the bond and affection between the bride and the groom ... and sometimes, the mother-in-law too!'

The group burst into laughter, nodding knowingly.

I let the laughter settle before continuing. 'But beyond the folklore, there's a very practical wisdom at play here. Mehendi is cooling in nature—it soothes the skin, calms the body and helps ease nerves before the big day. Imagine—on the surface, it's beauty, but underneath, it's medicine. Isn't that how love also works? It beautifies life, yes, but it also heals and calms us.'

I paused, as the group absorbed what I was saying. 'And there's one more lesson. Mehendi doesn't reveal its colour immediately. At first it looks pale, almost unimpressive. Only with time, warmth and stillness does the stain deepen into its full beauty. Love is the same. Its richness is not seen in the first flush of excitement alone but in the patience it takes to let it set, darken and grow over time.'

Everyone grew quiet, their smiles softening. A young cousin whispered, 'So the mehendi is not just for today, it's for the days ahead?'

I nodded. 'Exactly. Every ritual, when understood, becomes more than a mere custom—it becomes a mirror for life.'

Another guest, curious, asked, 'But Swamiji, why so many rituals? Doesn't religion seem full of them?'

I smiled. 'It does appear that way, doesn't it? But let me ask you something. Have you ever sung the birthday song for someone?'

Several heads nodded.

'Have you ever given a gift on a special occasion? Or offered flowers to someone you love? Or even sung a victory song when your favourite football team won?'

The group chuckled and nodded more vigorously.

'And why do we do these things?' I continued. 'Is the cake really needed? Couldn't we celebrate without gifts, without the flowers and the songs? Of course we could. But then how would the other person know what we feel? Rituals are not confined to religion. Life is full of them. They are the poetry through which the heart speaks. They are the grammar of love, joy and belonging.'

I let my words sink in. 'Now, look at the word "spiritual". It has its traditional meanings, of course. But here's a simple way of looking at it. The first three letters are "spi"—the spirit. The rest is "ritual". The spirit behind the ritual is to convey our genuine feelings. If the spirit is alive, the ritual becomes sacred. If the spirit is missing, what are we left with? Just ritual—empty, mechanical, routine.

'Think of how a birthday song sung without any feeling becomes noise. A "thank you" said without heart becomes formality. A "sorry" spoken without remorse becomes manipulation. The spirit makes all the difference.'

I gestured around us. 'Religions across cultures created rituals unique to their geography, their language, their history. One group lights a lamp, another rings a bell, another bows, another sings. But the purpose is the same—to express love, reverence and gratitude to the Divine. When the spirit was alive, religion was spiritual. But when the spirit fizzled out, we were left with only the shell—ritualistic religion. And that's when many stopped connecting, because the meaning and the feelings were lost. Yet, when the spirit is kept alive, religion and rituals can once again become a beautiful medium to connect with the Divine.'

The group grew silent, reflecting. The dholak beats picked up again, the children clapped in rhythm and the mehendi artists continued to weave their designs—pale at first but destined to turn a deeper and richer shade by morning.

As the laughter continued, the women weren't about to let the men escape. A group of cousins suddenly gathered around Rohan, who had been standing at the edge of the courtyard, pretending to be deeply invested in the dholak beats.

'*Arré, dulhe raja,*' one cousin teased, 'you think you'll get away? The mehendi is for you too!'

Rohan raised both hands in protest. 'No, no ... mehendi requires patience and steady hands. I barely survived tying my safa this morning. I'll clap, I'll dance—but mehendi, no chance!'

Lakshmi stepped in, smiling knowingly. 'Don't argue, beta. A little mehendi brings good fortune for the groom as well.'

Another cousin chimed in mischievously, 'At least let us write Sanjana's name in tiny font, somewhere hidden. Let's see if you can find it on your wedding night!'

Cheers erupted all around. I couldn't help but laugh watching Rohan's ears turn red. The poor boy was cornered. Finally, with an embarrassed grin, he held out his palm. A small, elegant design was etched on his hand—just his bride's initials tucked inside a swirl.

I smiled and said, 'Sometimes, surrender is the best victory, Rohan. Better to let the colour settle now than resist.'

He just shook his head, but his eyes betrayed the quiet pride of a groom-in-waiting.

As the mehendi cones moved and laughter filled the evening air, waiters appeared with large silver trays of steaming pakoras and kettles of masala chai. The aroma spread across the courtyard instantly—earthy, spicy, inviting. The pakoras were golden-brown, crisp at the edges, their crunchy exterior hiding tender slices of potato, onion and spinach within. Served with a splash of green chutney, they looked like little bundles of delicious warmth on a cool evening.

The guests eagerly reached out for the pakoras, only to realize their palms were covered in fresh mehendi. A chorus of frustrated groans and giggles followed.

'How do we eat now?' One woman laughed, holding up both her decorated hands helplessly.

At the centre of it all sat Sanjana, her hands beautifully painted, the henna still damp. She looked longingly at the pakoras but dared not move.

Rohan, watching, shook his head with mock seriousness. 'What kind of groom would I be if I let my bride starve?'

Then, with exaggerated care, he picked up a pakora, dipped it in the chutney and fed her. Sanjana's cheeks turned crimson as their friends whistled and clapped.

'Careful, Rohan,' one of them teased, 'if you keep this up, she'll expect room service every day after marriage!'

Even Dadi joined in the fun, waving her mehendi-stained palms. 'Beta, don't worry, after marriage, you won't just feed her pakoras—you'll be making them too!'

The courtyard rang with laughter as Rohan shook his head, smiling through his embarrassment.

Amidst all the teasing and chatter, one person sat quietly, smiling but never drawing attention to herself—Lakshmi. Everyone praised the palace chefs for the pakoras and tea. 'The resort's kitchen is just amazing,' a guest remarked, licking the last bit of chutney off his finger.

One of the butlers, beaming with pride, let it drop: 'Actually, these pakoras were Lakshmiji's recipe. She worked with the team in the kitchen this afternoon.'

A wave of surprise rippled through the courtyard. Heads turned. Hands clapped. Voices rose in admiration.

'Arré wah, Lakshmiji! Why didn't you say anything?'

'These are better than anything we've had in a five-star hotel!'

'You should start something of your own, seriously!'

Lakshmi, caught off-guard, blushed deeply. She raised her palms in protest. *'Arré, bas aise hi bana liye. Maine toh kabhi socha bhi nahi* [Oh, I just made them casually. I never even thought about it].'

From the corner, Rakesh, who had been quietly sipping his tea, suddenly piped up, his eyes twinkling, 'If she starts a business, the world will enjoy ... and we will starve!'

There was a burst of laughter. Lakshmi smacked his arm lightly, shaking her head. 'See, this is why I never even think of it!'

∼

Watching Lakshmi, I thought to myself: People like her are like salt. Salt adds immense value to any preparation, yet no one ever sees it. No one praises the salt, they praise the dish. We only realize its worth when it's missing.

This reminded me of one such person in our temple community: Padmavati Devi Dasi. A nurse by profession, she spent her days caring for patients, and every evening—no matter how tired she was, come rain or shine—she would bring fresh jasmine flowers to the temple with her own money. With delicate hands, she would spend hours crafting bracelets, anklets and garlands for our deities, Sri Sri Radha Gopinath.

She did not do this for recognition or applause, but as an act of devotion—a quiet labour of love that continued for over three decades.

And the truth was that most of us took it for granted. The jasmine bracelets were always there, always perfect, always fragrant. Like salt, her service blended so seamlessly into the offering that we forgot to see the one who was making it possible.

A couple of years ago, during the grand celebration of the deities' appearance day—Brahmotsavam—we decided to honour those 'salt-like' devotees whose service was invisible yet indispensable. Naturally, we thought of Padmavati Devi Dasi. We planned to interview her, though we knew she would be shy, reluctant to step into the spotlight.

But when we went to her, we discovered something heartbreaking. She was suffering from severe dementia and other health complications. With no family to care for her, she had been struggling silently for a long time.

We couldn't record a fresh interview. Instead, we used old footage of her making jasmine ornaments with those steady hands of devotion. When the video was played to thousands of devotees, many wept. To see the quiet givers finally recognized touched something deep in all of us. In that moment, our community also rallied. Some members came forward to take care of her.

We were left with one piercing question at the end of the experience: Why did we wait so long? Why should it take decades, or an illness, or absence, for us to finally say 'thank you' to someone? Sometimes, delaying appreciation can mean never having the chance to say it at all.

A word spoken today, an acknowledgement offered right now can be life-changing for those who quietly give everything they have.

Think about it for a moment, dear friends—who's the salt in your life? Perhaps it's your grandparents, your parents, your spouse or that quiet colleague who holds everything together without ever asking for appreciation. Homes and workplaces are full of such 'salt-like' individuals—quiet, steady givers who keep adding value, who bring flavour without fuss, but who rarely receive the acknowledgement they deserve. And sadly, when they step away, only then does everyone recognize what they brought to the table in the first place.

We must learn to notice and appreciate the salt while it's still there—acknowledge the quiet contributors, celebrate their consistency and give them the dignity of being seen. A simple 'thank you' on time can sometimes be worth more than a hundred praises given too late.

Being humble is beautiful, but humility doesn't mean invisibility. Salt doesn't have to overpower the dish, but neither must it dissolve without a trace. Like introverts learning to express themselves a little more, or extroverts learning to listen a little better, even salt-like people can step forward occasionally to voice their needs, to share their ideas, to remind others that they are present.

I am reminded of a dear friend of mine in the ashram, also a monk. He was the very definition of salt—steady, dependable, always ready to serve. Whatever the need, whatever the hour, he would simply say yes. And you know how it is, right? '*Jo kare, woh aur kare, aur karta rahe, aur zindagi bhar karte-karte mare* [The one who always does ends up doing more, until doing becomes their whole life].' He was that person—the one you could lean on without hesitation, knowing he would never let you down.

He was also very responsible in his service, and was part of the temple's management when I was a part of it too. He had great ideas, sharp insights and a clarity of thought that could have benefited everyone. But since he had a salt-like personality, he preferred to stay quiet during meetings. Shy and a little apprehensive of being judged by the doyens around the table, he would swallow his thoughts and let others speak. And I often noticed that he was used by people. Not in a malicious way, but because everyone knew he would never say no.

One day, I sat him down for a conversation. I told him, 'Sometimes, saying no is not an unwillingness to serve—it is simply drawing the right boundaries to protect your self-respect.'

And then I reminded him of a truth worth holding close:

Give. But don't allow yourself to be used.
Love. But don't allow your heart to be abused.
Trust. But don't be naive.
Listen. But don't lose your own voice.

Service is sacred, yes. But silence is not always golden. If he had brilliant ideas—and he did—he had to learn to share them. Even if people questioned him, even if some didn't accept his thoughts, that was fine. At least his voice would be heard.

He listened quietly. It wasn't easy for him. But gradually, with gentle encouragement and a little prodding, he began to change. He started speaking up in meetings. He began to say no without feeling guilty when his plate was already full. And to his surprise, people respected him more for it.

Today, he is still the same steady, dependable monk—still salt—but now he knows his worth. His ideas shape decisions, his voice adds strength and his presence is both felt and valued.

That's what I mean when I say salt should be the hero ingredient and should sometimes step out and shine. Goodness should not mean being neglected, being used or becoming a doormat. Goodness deserves dignity.

True balance is when contribution is recognized and expression is encouraged. For when salt knows its worth, and others honour it, every dish—and every relationship—becomes richer.

Watching Lakshmi shrink from the spotlight, I realized how many people live like this.

Kuch log apnon ke liye sapnon se door rehte hai, aur kuch log sapnon ke liye apnon se door rehte hai.

Some people quietly set aside their own space, choices or comfort to be there for their loved ones. Others step away from their loved ones to chase their dreams.

Who is right? Who is wrong? The truth is: neither. Each person's life journey is unique, as are the choices they make. We often see sacrificing our dreams for our loved ones as an expression of love, but choosing to pursue those dreams can be another form of love too.

The real art is in knowing when to hold back and when to step forward. For those like Lakshmi, who have lived their years for others, maybe life is whispering now: It's time to give a little space to your own dreams too. Because a life spent only in sacrifice is a life half-lived. Sometimes even salt deserves to sparkle.

I saw this play out in my own family. After my father passed away, a kind family friend visited my mother and gave her a piece of advice that transformed her life. He told her gently, 'You've always lived for others—first for your parents, then for your husband, then for your children. Your son is a monk—busy in his own world of travelling and teaching. Your daughter is married and has her own family, busy in her responsibilities. You cared for your ailing husband for so many years. In giving so much to others, you forgot to live for yourself. Don't stop caring for your children, don't become selfish—but now it's time to also live the way you want to, do the things you love.'

Being a financial consultant, our well-wisher added a practical twist to his counsel: 'Every month, whatever income comes in—your pension and from other sources—save enough for contingencies and emergencies by investing wisely. But the rest? Spend it fully on yourself. Don't carry a single penny into the next month. Use it for what makes you happy.'

My mother took that advice to heart. She still cares deeply for her family and community, but now she also lives fully for herself. She has gone back to cooking with passion—not just for us, but for others too. Every day, she prepares a meal for over twenty monks in her temple community, making sure each plate is served with love. She keeps cooking, sharing, experimenting and spreading joy through her food.

And she's also rediscovered another old love. When we were children, she would read one novel a day. She was a voracious, curious and insatiable reader. Then life pulled her away from it—first it was the responsibilities at home, then helping my father financially as the breadwinner, then caring for him during his illness. After his passing, she returned to reading, but this time she dived into spiritual literature. Today she can spend eight to ten hours a day reading. She reads a book a day with the same hunger she had as a girl, except now it nourishes her soul as much as her mind.

That, dear friends, is the secret to a fulfilling life. Sacrifice is a must—it is the virtue that keeps families, friendships and communities going. But sacrifice alone is not enough. It must be balanced with self-care and joy, with doing something that lights up *our* spirit too. Living only for ourselves makes us selfish, but living only for others can leave us empty. We have to find a balance between the two.

Sacrifice keeps love alive. Passion keeps *us* alive.

I looked at her gently and said, 'Lakshmiji, you've spent years adding flavour to everyone else's lives. Maybe it's time to serve your own recipe to the world.'

A cousin added, grinning, 'We'll be your first customers—lifetime subscription to pakoras!'

More laughter followed. Even Priya joined in: 'Careful, Ma, once you start, even the palace chefs might apply for jobs under you! But seriously ... all your life you've fed us. Maybe this is life's way of telling you it's time to feed your passion for cooking even more.'

The courtyard buzzed with encouragement, teasing banter and applause. Lakshmi, overwhelmed, blushed again. Finally, with a shy smile and eyes shimmering, she whispered, '*Theek hai* ... Maybe.'

And in that moment, something changed. The glow of sacrifice she had worn all her life was now embellished with another glow—the glow of dreams finally daring to breathe.

While the applause around Lakshmi diminished, Ved still sat quietly in a corner, absorbed in sketching, lost in details others missed—motifs inspired by the mehendi, caricatures of the guests laughing, eating pakoras, tiny flourishes that brought the pages alive.

When someone mischievously snatched the sketchbook and began passing it around, the courtyard erupted in exclamations.

'Ved, these are brilliant!'

'Look at this one—he's even captured Dadi's mehendi!'

'Beta, you're gifted!'

Everyone admired his art. Everyone except Priya. Her smile was there but it was weighed down. Praise filled the air, but her silence felt heavier than all of it.

Ved looked at her directly. 'Mom, you don't look too happy.'

Priya lowered her eyes. 'I am proud, Ved. Truly. But …' She hesitated, struggling for words. 'Your dad once said, "You and I will design, and when Ved grows up, if he studies business and leads the firm, our brand will rock." It was his dream. Sometimes I wonder if I owe it to him … and to you.'

Ved's jaw tightened. He looked away. 'But what if his dream isn't mine?'

The impact of the words was deeply felt. The courtyard grew still.

Rakesh, who had been watching silently, finally spoke, 'Ved, I also dream that you'll join me one day. Run the family business. Build on what we've worked for. Isn't that what every grandfather hopes for?'

Ved pressed his lips together. He was torn between his desires and his family's expectations. His voice cracked as he turned to me. 'So what do I do, Gaurji? Please them … or myself? Honour everyone's dream for me … except my own?'

His words carried the weight of countless young hearts.

I stepped forward and placed a hand gently on his shoulder. 'Ved, you see expectations as a cage. But look again—they are also an embrace. Your nani has always lived for her family, out of love. Your mother carries your father's dream, out of love. Your grandfather offers his business to you, out of love. None of them want to trap you. They only want to secure you.'

Ved blinked, divided. His eyes darted to Priya.

'But Swamiji … if he makes the wrong choice? If he suffers?' said Priya.

I smiled. 'Then he will learn. Just as you did when you chose fashion against the odds, Priya. Just as you did, Rakeshji, when you built your business from scratch. Experience is a better teacher than safety.'

Rakesh grumbled, half-serious, half-loving. 'Hmph. Easy to say. But passion doesn't pay the bills.'

The group chuckled, the tension easing slightly.

'True, Rakeshji,' I said with a smile, 'but nor does an unlived life. Stability feeds the body, yes. But passion feeds the soul. Ved will need both. And with your wisdom beside him, he can learn to balance the two.'

Turning to Ved, I continued, 'Sometimes, we are fortunate enough to study or take up a course that aligns with our passion. But if we are already walking another path, that doesn't mean the passion has to die. You can complete what you've started, and still nurture your calling on the side. As your nanu rightly said, passion doesn't always pay the bills in the beginning. For now, you have the privilege of your family's support until your passion begins to sustain you. Risks are important—they give life meaning—but the wisest risks are the ones taken with preparation, and not on an impulse.'

I paused and softened my tone. 'And for those who don't have that privilege, there is still a way out. A career that pays the bills can offer stability. You can pursue your passion alongside it—not for money at first, but to refine it, build it and keep it alive. If life is kind and your efforts steady, one day that passion may grow into a career too. That, Ved, is balance—it's not about dropping everything for a dream, but about weaving duty and desire into the same fabric of life.'

Ved looked up, eyes shimmering. 'So you're saying … I don't have to reject them or myself. I can carry their love and still follow my art?'

I nodded. 'Exactly. Their dreams can guide you, but they don't have to define you. You can honour them by succeeding—not in their way, but in yours.'

Rakesh sighed, shaking his head in mock defeat. 'Bas, one condition—if you become a famous artist, your first exhibition better be sponsored by my business!'

The courtyard erupted in laughter. Priya's eyes glistened as she smiled at her son, and Lakshmi's proud glance at her grandson said what words could not.

∽

As I watched Ved struggle, I realized that this dilemma is common to many families.

Every parent has big dreams for their child. They have lived longer, seen more, suffered more. Their hopes are stitched with the threads of care and concern. To dismiss them outright would not only be unwise, it would be arrogant. After all, a parent's dream is rarely born from selfishness—it is born from love.

But every child also has their own rhythm. A spark that is uniquely theirs. To completely suppress that spark for the sake of someone else's dream is to smother the very soul of a human being. What kind of life would it be where your heartbeat is dictated entirely by another?

So what do we do when parents' dreams and children's desires collide? The answer, I believe, lies in empathy—on both sides.

Children must learn to honour their parents' intentions, to see that behind every expectation is love, not control. Parents want their children to 'be safe' because they know how difficult the world can be.

Parents, too, must honour their children's individuality. Love does not mean converting your child into a replica of yourself. True love allows freedom—the freedom to grow in a different direction, the freedom to make mistakes and also discover one's own truth.

Balance is found not in silence but in conversation. Sometimes a child may choose to carry forward a parent's dream, but in their own style. Sometimes the child must walk a completely different road. Yet even then, they can still carry their family's values with them like a compass guiding them in the right direction.

It's like a symphony where the different generations play together—the seasoned bring rhythm, wisdom and steadiness, while the young contribute energy, curiosity and spark. When both find harmony together, the music becomes fuller, deeper—something no solo performance could ever create.

Parents' dreams are stitched with care, wisdom and protection. They have weathered life through all its seasons, and simply want their children to carry an umbrella. Children's dreams are stitched with passion, individuality and hope. They long to dance in the rain, feel the world for themselves—even if it means getting drenched.

So what happens when the child doesn't want to carry the umbrella? Yes, conflict arises. But within that conflict lies the opportunity to understand one another more deeply, to meld security with passion and wisdom with individuality.

The richest inheritance one can receive is not merely dreams or a sense of duty, but the wisdom to balance both. Stability without passion can leave us safe but hollow. Passion without stability can leave us excited but adrift. Together, they make life both secure *and* soulful.

∽

The courtyard pulsed with music, merriment and the aroma of hot samosas, as one of Sanjana's closest friends hurried over, her face glowing with excitement. 'Sanju, Rohan! You won't believe this—my very good friend Karan, the one I used to work with? He's here in Jaisalmer for a project and is staying at this resort! If I remember correctly, you were in the same college as him, weren't you, Sanju?'

Sanjana gave a small nod, her smile polite but somewhat terse.

'I thought, why not have him drop by? Didn't want to bother you, Sanju, so I checked with Gaurav Bhaiya, who checked with Rakesh Uncle and Lakshmi Aunty—they were perfectly fine with it, so I invited him too!'

Karan walked in behind her. Tall, broad-shouldered and impeccably dressed, with the easy confidence of someone who knew his presence filled a room. His handshake was firm, his smile effortless—the kind that turned heads without trying.

Rohan stood up to warmly greet Karan. 'Welcome! Always nice to have more friends join the celebration.'

But Sanjana … was frozen. Her face was drained of all colour. Her lips parted, as if to speak, but no words emerged. She lowered her eyes quickly, adjusting her dupatta as though it could shield her.

For the briefest moment, Karan's eyes flickered—an unspoken recognition, sharp and clear—but in the next breath, he masked it with charm. 'Congratulations to both of you! Beautiful ceremony.'

His words were light, almost casual. Sanjana's friends, oblivious, cheered and clapped, pulling Karan into introductions. The courtyard filled up again with laughter and music, the rhythm resuming as though nothing had shifted.

Only Sanjana's hand trembled slightly, making the mehendi artist chuckle as the mehendi cone slipped a little: 'Don't move too much, or the pattern will smudge.'

The moment passed, swallowed by the noise of the celebration. Yet, like the first pale trace of mehendi that deepens in colour with time, something unspoken lingered— waiting to show its true shade.

As I looked around that evening, the courtyard throbbed with laughter and light—brass lamps flickering in the desert breeze, children darting between the chairs and the air fragrant with the smell of jasmine. Rohan sat nearby, blushing, as his friends teased him about his bride's initials hidden within a swirl of mehendi, while Gaurav and Dadi argued cheerfully over whose flower design looked prettier.

And then there was Sanjana—composed, still … almost too still. Her hands rested lightly on her lap, the mehendi darkening to a deeper brown, but her gaze wasn't on it. Every so often, her eyes drifted towards the edge of the courtyard— not searching exactly, but as if pulled by a thought she couldn't shake off.

Karan stood a little apart, surrounded by conversation, yet not quite in it. His laughter came half a second late, his posture too casual, as though rehearsed. And once—just once—their eyes met across the crowd. It was fleeting, but it carried a charge that didn't belong in this joyous night.

That's when I felt it—a faint dissonance in the air, like a note slightly out of tune in an otherwise-perfect melody. Everyone else swayed to the rhythm of the celebration; only these two seemed to be counting a different beat.

I couldn't have said what it was then—a memory, a regret, a story unfinished—but I knew a new song had filled the courtyard that the music could not drown out. The night still laughed, but beneath the mirth, something had begun to shift.

....

THINGS TO THINK ABOUT ...

THE SALT WITHIN: Some people are like salt—invisible yet indispensable. They add flavour to life without seeking recognition. True wisdom is twofold—to learn to value such 'salt-like' contributors while they are still with us, and for those people to know their worth and allow their presence to shine.

A BALANCE OF DUTY AND DESIRE: Life often pulls us between responsibilities and dreams. Some step away from personal aspirations to serve family, others leave family behind to chase their dreams. Neither is right or wrong. Everyone walks a different path. Life doesn't have one right answer—sometimes, love means giving our dreams up, and sometimes it means chasing them with all our heart. Duty gives us stability, dreams give us vitality. Together, they create a harmonious life.

RISKY PASSION VS STABLE CAREER: If we are financially privileged, we can pursue something that aligns with our passion by taking calculated—not impulsive—risks. If we are not financially comfortable, a stable career can provide security while our passion is nurtured on the side. And when effort meets opportunity, that passion might slowly blossom into our life's work.

CONFLICTING DREAMS: Parents dream in the language of protection, shaping paths that feel safe and certain. Children dream in the language of possibility, chasing horizons that promise more. When these two languages clash, misunderstandings arise—but so does the opportunity to translate love into understanding, and care into freedom.

....

The exercises related to the concepts mentioned in this chapter can be found on p. 269.

6

Standing Still within a Storm

Building Your Foundations of Inner Strength

~

Love does not vanish in the shadows, it deepens when we dare to bring the shadows into light.

Soon after the mehendi festivities, the preparations for the evening's sangeet began in full force. The courtyard echoed with the melody of Bollywood tracks as the cousins practised their dance steps, their laughter louder than the beats of the dhol. Some groaned about aching feet, others fought over the choreography, while self-appointed 'directors' corrected hand movements as if they were staging a Broadway show. The whole palace had become a rehearsal hall alive with music, fun and nervous excitement.

I slipped away into one of the secluded palace gardens. A fountain bubbled gently in the centre, surrounded by rose bushes heavy with blooms and medieval stone benches that must have been privy to centuries of secrets. The faint sound of chatter drifted over the walls—a reminder of the chaos I had stepped away from. Here, there was peace.

But I wasn't alone for long.

Sanjana walked in, her dupatta catching the breeze like a reluctant kite. Her eyes scanned the garden until they rested on me. She paused, and then approached with a smile that looked carefully placed—the kind people wear when their heart is elsewhere.

'Swamiji,' she began softly, 'I just wanted to ask if you've been comfortable here at the resort. Everyone's been so busy, I don't think anyone has been able to check with you.'

I replied, 'Very comfortable, Sanjana—perhaps a little *too* comfortable. You see, a monk's biggest challenge isn't discomfort, it's getting too used to comfort.'

That earned a laugh from her.

I added, smiling, 'And yes, Rakeshji, Lakshmiji, Ved, Priya, and your brother, Gaurav, have all been checking in on me—not only to see if I need anything but to keep me wonderfully entertained. Between their stories and their company, I haven't had a single dull moment.'

'I was worried people might be troubling you too much, coming to you with their issues, asking for guidance.' She smiled.

'Not at all,' I replied. 'That's an occupational hazard for monks. Just like how pilots can't complain about turbulence, we can't complain about people opening their hearts to us. Honestly, it's always a joy to be of some service.'

Sanjana smiled and lowered herself onto the bench opposite me. Her eyes lingered on the mehendi staining her palms. The intricate designs were darkening slowly. When she spoke, her voice came out faint, uneven, like a flute played on a broken breath.

'Swamiji, I want to tell you something,' she said, looking straight at me—not searching for approval, just ready to speak. 'I was in junior college when I first met Karan. If you remember, he arrived unexpectedly during the mehendi. He had ... he had this energy, this way of walking into a room and making you believe you were the only one there. And he was handsome. Everyone noticed him—but he noticed me. His attention felt like sunlight breaking through the clouds.'

Sanjana's lips curved into a small, bittersweet smile that flickered, then faded away.

'At first it was magic. Long drives, stolen coffees between lectures, late-night conversations that made me believe love could conquer anything. He was ambitious, bold, so full of dreams. And I … I thought I'd be a part of those dreams.'

Her eyes grew distant, her jaw tightening. 'From a distance, everything felt perfect. But when you're inside it … storms aren't so romantic, are they? Karan's charm—it came with pride. His passion could fill a room, but sometimes it left no space for my voice.'

She looked down, her eyes wet. I could see her fighting the tears, not letting them spill.

As she looked away, she said, 'I thought I had moved on. I told myself I was stronger without him, that some loves are meant to be lessons, not last for a lifetime. But this morning … seeing him walk into the courtyard, smiling as if no time had passed … It felt like I had seen a ghost.'

She exhaled sharply, as if the very act of admitting to her feelings out loud had calmed the turmoil she'd been caught in. The garden air seemed to grow stiller around her. I remained silent, leaning slightly forward, my hands folded—not to interrupt, but to hold the space she clearly needed.

After a pause, Sanjana continued, 'And then there's Rohan … He's so different. I first met him at King's College in London. I was juggling a stack of books on a staircase after class—typical me, late for something. And there he was. He didn't swoop in with a line or his charm, he just quietly took a couple of books from me and said, "Careful, the top one's about to fall." That was it.

'He didn't dazzle me with fireworks, he grounded me with warmth. He didn't talk over me, he listened. He didn't promise me the stars—he reminded me that even everyday moments could be extraordinary.'

Her expression softened, the memory brightening it up. 'Later, we became friends—study groups, chats between classes, long walks along the Thames when the city felt too heavy. With Karan, I was always running, breathless, trying to keep up. With Rohan, I slowed down. I was steady. Safe. Seen.'

Her voice lowered, trembling but clear, she said, 'That's why I fell in love with him. That's why I said yes when he proposed. Because for the first time, I wasn't just in love—I was at peace. Rohan became more than just my partner ... he became my anchor. My soulmate.'

She pressed her palms together, the mehendi dark against her skin. 'And yet ... Karan's sudden presence has unsettled me. Not because I still love him—I don't. But because the heart doesn't always obey the mind. Memories creep in, uninvited. And I fear what Rohan must have seen on my face. I fear what he must be thinking now.'

Her eyes, finally meeting mine, pleaded silently for assurance, for clarity and release. I said nothing, only nodded slightly—enough to tell her she was heard. Sometimes silence is the only response worthy of a heart in unrest.

The faint sound of dhol beats and friends and cousins' laughter drifted in from the sangeet rehearsals, cruelly cheerful, mocking the turmoil in Sanjana's chest. She held out her palms, still damp with henna, and whispered, 'The mehendi is supposed to darken with time, isn't it? A sign of love growing deeper. But what if Karan's arrival has smudged mine before it can set properly?'

The garden fell quiet. Birds dipped into the fountain and rose again. The fragrance of roses hung in the still air. Sanjana sat with her eyes lowered, waiting—for words, for solace, for something that might steady her trembling heart.

I looked at her, my voice gentle, and said, 'Sanjana, I may not know the exact weight of what you're carrying, but I can feel the heaviness of your heart. And I want you to know it's okay. It's okay to feel shaken when the past suddenly stands before you. It doesn't mean you are weak, and it certainly doesn't mean your present is any less real. It only means you are human.'

Her eyes flickered, and a tear she had been holding back finally slipped free.

'The human heart—whether in marriage, friendship or devotion—is fragile in the same way. What you are experiencing is very natural. The past has a way of knocking on the door, especially when we least expect it. But remember, when someone from our past appears, they don't necessarily bring love back with them. They bring memories. And memories are tricky—they can feel alive even when the love itself is long gone.'

I leaned forward, my words slower now, deliberate. 'Karan was your storm. He swept you into moments that felt larger than life. He taught you lessons, left you with memories and shaped a part of who you are today. But Rohan is your harbour. With him, you have found steadiness, peace and the rare gift of being truly seen. Storms dazzle from a distance, but they are exhausting and dangerous up-close. Fireworks can light up the sky for a moment, but ultimately they vanish.'

Sanjana wiped her eyes with the edge of her dupatta, listening intently, her breathing calmer now.

'And about your fear ...' I added softly. 'If Rohan noticed something, don't let it frighten you. Instead, let it become an opportunity to be honest. Shadows grow larger in silence. But when you bring them into light, they shrink. Speak to him, not to burden him, but to strengthen what you already share—your bond. Real love isn't afraid of truth. It doesn't break in the face of honesty, it deepens.'

I glanced at her mehendi-stained palms. 'And as for the smudge you fear—remember, even the most intricate mehendi often smears here and there. That doesn't ruin the design. It only makes it unique. What matters is not whether the mehendi is flawless, but whether the colour deepens. And the way I see it, your colour with Rohan is still deepening.'

For a while, Sanjana was silent. Finally, she exhaled and said, 'Swamiji ... you're right. Karan brought back memories, not love. My present and future are with Rohan. Like I said before, he is my anchor. I cannot let yesterday's shadow steal tomorrow's light.' A gentle smile touched her lips. 'I will speak to him—with honesty. If this bond is to last, it must stand in the light, not hide in the shadow of secrecy. It must rest on truth, not silence. Thank you ... for listening, and for helping me listen to myself.'

She rose from the bench, adjusting her dupatta, feeling a little lighter than before.

As she walked back towards the palace, the fading sunlight caught her decorated hands. The patterns had grown darker, the hues richer. A quiet reminder that love, too, deepens when it is lived openly, without concealment.

∼

I often share this little joke. A married man once went to a well-known sadhu and said, 'Maharaj, I have so many problems in my marriage. Please give me a solution.' The sadhu looked at him kindly and replied, 'Come on, my dear! If I had the solution to this particular problem, why do you think I became a sadhu in the first place?'

It always gets a laugh. But behind the humour lies a very real question that people often ask me: 'Swamiji, you're a monk. You've never been in a romantic relationship, never been married. Then how can you advise us about marriage and relationships?'

It's a fair question. Let me answer it in parts.

For years I lived with over eighty monks in the ashram. Now, you might imagine that a monastery is full of serene, saintly men who agree on everything and float around in peace all day. The reality? Put eighty human beings together—even if they're renunciants—and you'll still find egos, differing temperaments, clashing opinions and the occasional cold war over whose turn it is to clean the temple hall. It's still community life, and community life means navigating different personalities. Learning to adjust, to communicate, to forgive, to respect differences—these are the same principles that apply in every relationship, whether it's between spouses, friends or colleagues. The flavours may differ, but the ingredients are the same.

Secondly, over the years, countless people have opened up their hearts to me. I have listened to stories of heartbreaks and divorces, of conflicts between husband and wife, misunderstandings between parents and children, jealousies between siblings and even betrayals between close friends. Each story left me with not just sympathy but insight—perspectives about human behaviour, patterns that repeat across generations and lessons that are evergreen and widely applicable.

Add to that my study of ancient scriptures and literature. Our traditions are filled with wisdom on how to live, love, forgive and grow. These texts may be centuries old, but the human heart hasn't changed all that much. Our technology is modern, our lifestyles are faster, but our needs—to be seen, valued, respected and loved—remain timeless.

And then, when I am asked how I can advise you all on matters of the heart, I often say with a smile: 'Perhaps some of this experience comes from my previous lives, stored in my subconscious, resurfacing at the right time when someone needs to hear it.'

So while I may not have walked the road of marriage myself, I have walked alongside thousands who have. And in listening deeply, reflecting sincerely and studying carefully, I have found that the principles of relationships are universal. The details vary, but the truths remain the same.

Relationships are like a building. What we usually admire is the external structure—the architecture, the design, the height that touches the sky. But the real factor that determines whether that building can endure is something we don't see—the foundation.

A structure can look magnificent on the outside, but if its foundation is weak, the first rough wind, the first tremor, the first heavy rain can bring it down. On the other hand, even if the walls crack or the paint peels, if the foundation is solid, the building can be repaired, restored or even rebuilt to stand tall again.

It is the same with relationships.

The external form of a relationship is easy to be swept away by the attraction, the chemistry, the social image of being the 'perfect couple'. These are like the shiny walls and polished windows of a tall building. They matter, yes, but they are not what will hold you when life shakes you.

The foundation of a relationship is different. It is built of things far less glamorous but infinitely more essential:

- **Trust:** The quiet assurance that your partner will stand by you even when the world doesn't.
- **Respect:** Not just admiring strengths but also honouring differences, knowing that individuality does not threaten togetherness.
- **Communication:** The ability to speak honestly and listen empathetically, especially when it is uncomfortable.
- **Shared Values:** Common principles and life directions that become the compass when emotions run wild.
- **Commitment:** The strength to choose the bond again and again, not only when it is easy, but when it is difficult.

Think of how cities are designed.

If we don't start with the invisible groundwork—the sewage, drainage, wiring and circuit protections—a tiny electrical fault or a blocked drain can cascade into a fire or a flood. It's not a single spark or rain that destroys a city but the gaps in its unseen systems.

A relationship works the same way. The unseen infrastructure—trust, values, communication—determines whether it can withstand the pressures that life inevitably brings. There will be upheavals—misunderstandings, failures, financial struggles, health issues, even betrayals. Walls may crack. Windows may shatter. The external structure might take a hit. But if the foundation is strong, you can repair, restore and rebuild. Like a well-built city that survives its monsoons and still lights up every night, love, too, can endure the rough seasons—evolving, expanding and sometimes even growing stronger in the process.

The problem in today's world is that too many people get carried away by the external structure. Somewhere between physical infatuation and momentary pleasure, love gets lost. Many relationships are built like a house of cards—beautiful when stacked, fragile when touched. When the external beauty fades, or when reality intrudes, the whole thing collapses because there was no foundation beneath.

True love is not built on candlelight dinners alone, it is built on the basis of how you handle disagreements. It is not proven only by holding hands in public, but by holding each other through private pain. It is not defined by how quickly two hearts race together, but by how patiently two souls grow together.

And this truth doesn't apply only to marriage—it applies to every bond we have, whether with friends, family, colleagues or even with ourselves.

So if you are in a relationship, ask yourself—are you decorating the walls, or are you strengthening the foundation? Because beauty is fleeting, but stability allows beauty to keep returning, again and again, no matter how many challenges life sends your way.

But let me return to Sanjana's predicament for a moment. One of the greatest challenges, dear readers, that often haunts any relationship is a fractured past. It may be between a father and daughter, like Priya and Rakesh, or between partners, like Sanjana and Karan. It could just as easily exist between siblings, friends, colleagues or even within communities. Unless there is genuine healing that allows one to move on, the past has a way of resurfacing. It doesn't always come back as a full-blown event—sometimes it returns as subtle triggers, painful memories or tricky situations that can quietly steal our peace, joy and even jeopardize the present.

I once heard a monk share a very profound principle. He explained that while we often *think* we have healed or moved on, in reality, we sometimes continue to feed our traumas internally. We may not speak of them, but inside, we keep replaying the old tapes—regretting, brooding or even nurturing hidden resentment and anger. Each time we do so, we are vibrating at the same internal frequency as the pain we claim to have left behind externally. And ironically, that very vibration attracts either the same kind of treatment, similar patterns or even the same kind of people into our lives.

This brings me to the very interesting story about a girl who kept meeting the same person over and over again.

This young woman came to me in frustration. She had been in two failed relationships, and in both cases the men displayed shockingly similar traits—they were emotionally unavailable, dismissive of her needs and somewhat manipulative. When she finally stepped into a third relationship, she was startled. Not only did the guy share the same negative patterns, he even shared the same first name as her last partner.

She asked me, 'Why does this keep happening? Why does every person I meet turn out the same?'

The truth is, she wasn't just meeting the same kind of person by accident. She was unconsciously attracting them. Internally, she was still carrying the unhealed wounds from her earlier relationships. Every time she entered a new one, those wounds whispered into her ears a story of fear and doubt. That inner energy shaped her choices, blinded her to the red flags and almost magnetically pulled her towards men who would treat her in the same poor way. Until she consciously healed those wounds, she would keep repeating the loop.

And then there is the young man who had grown up with a father who always criticized him. Nothing he did was ever good enough. Over the years, this chipped away at his self-confidence. By the time he was an adult, he carried this belief deep within: I am not worthy. I am not capable.

This inner script reflected in his life. His girlfriend treated him dismissively, his boss overlooked his contributions and his colleagues subtly undermined him. It wasn't that the world had singled him out unfairly—it was his own energy and conditioning shaping the way others responded to him.

Unless he stopped feeding that old energy and started wiring himself differently, he would continue to attract the same behaviour from the world. The first step was for him to recognize that his father's criticism was not his truth. True healing involved affirming his worth, building new internal scripts and choosing relationships that reflected respect rather than repeating old wounds.

In light of both these stories, we can see that external efforts are always needed to help us improve ourselves and move ahead. We might have to work on communication, mediation, conflict resolution and other practical aspects of relationships. These certainly help. And in extreme cases, we may even need to seek new partners, new jobs or healthier surroundings. But unless our internal energy changes, all external efforts will have little or no lasting value.

To rise above painful patterns, we need more than external change—we need an inner shift. The acronym A-R-I-S-E offers a step-by-step compass:

A – Awareness

The first step is simply to notice the pattern. What keeps repeating in your life? Do you often find yourself in relationships where you give more than you receive? Or in jobs where your effort is overlooked and your voice goes unheard? Do friendships fade when you start setting boundaries? Do you find yourself always being dismissed, undervalued and not chosen? Awareness shines the light on cycles we otherwise stumble through in the dark.

The young woman who had unhappy relationships with men who showed the same traits had to pause and ask herself: 'Why does this story keep replaying?' It was awareness that helped her to start healing.

R – Release and Heal

Awareness is powerful, but unless we release old emotions, they will keep recycling within us. Healing means allowing ourselves to feel regret, anger or grief—and then to let them go. It is not about forgetting the past, but about no longer letting it control us.

The young man criticized by his father carried that disapproval like a wound. His girlfriend, his boss, his colleagues all seemed to echo it. Healing for him meant acknowledging the pain and consciously releasing it, instead of reliving it daily.

I – Install New Scripts

Old inner scripts like 'I am not enough' or 'This is all I deserve' must be deliberately replaced with new affirmations and beliefs: 'I am worthy of love and respect. I am capable.' Each time the old story resurfaces, we install a new one to override it.

For the young man, catching himself when he thought 'I'll never be good enough' and replacing it with 'I have value' was the work of rewiring. Slowly, he began responding differently—and others responded differently to him.

S – Set Boundaries

Healing doesn't mean tolerating what hurts us. Boundaries are a form of self-respect. They are not walls to shut people out but gates that let in only what nourishes us.

For the young woman, learning to say 'This doesn't work for me' when her needs were ignored was an act of courage. Without that, the cycle would have repeated endlessly.

E – Energy Shift

Finally, we need to shift our energy towards clarity, peace and self-respect. Healing changes how we see ourselves, and that in turn changes what we attract. When we surround ourselves with healthier influences, the world responds differently.

For Sanjana, when Karan suddenly reappeared in her life, she struggled, which is only natural. Old wounds had been stirred. But thanks to her healed self, timely guidance and a healthier circle of well-wishers around her, she responded gracefully. What was different was not Karan, but Sanjana's energy. She had broken out of the old loop.

Breaking the loop is not about erasing the past but about choosing to A-R-I-S-E above it:

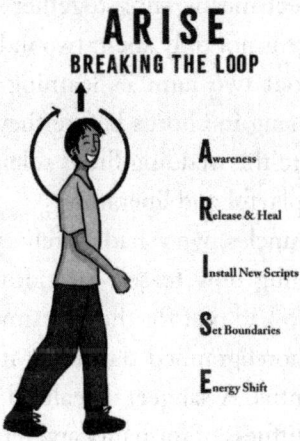

ARISE
BREAKING THE LOOP

Awareness

Release & Heal

Install New Scripts

Set Boundaries

Energy Shift

And always remember: We don't move on by forgetting. We move on by remembering differently—without rehearsing the hurt.

~

By twilight, the palace had dressed itself in vibrant colours and gold. Strings of lights draped across domes, the courtyard glowed like a jewel and the air buzzed with dhol beats, laughter and a hint of mischief. Guests gathered, chattering excitedly, their phones ready to capture every moment.

The dance floor was crowded, the beats irresistible and even the shyest guests found themselves clapping in rhythm. For a moment, I stepped aside, watching the colours swirl and the laughter echo through the palace courtyard.

It struck me then—why do we have a sangeet in weddings at all? Surely, the sacred vows and solemn rituals of marriage should be enough. But then again, life is not only about vows and rituals. It is also about music and play.

The word sangeet means 'sung together'. And that is its essence. A marriage is not only about two individuals coming together—it is about two families learning to share joy, to laugh together, to sing in chorus before they stand together in ceremony. Where the wedding fire is solemn and binding, the sangeet fire is playful and liberating.

I watched as uncles who had barely spoken to each other in the morning now teased each other in song, and distant cousins who had met for the first time only yesterday now performed choreographed dances as if they had been rehearsing for months. A sangeet, I realized, breaks barriers. It takes away the stiffness of formality and replaces it with the warmth of shared laughter.

Traditional songs once carried deeper meanings—teasing the groom, blessing the bride, expressing the ache of separation and the joy of new beginnings. Today, Bollywood has replaced these touching folk songs, but the essence remains the same—to tell a story, to celebrate love, to transform the weight of change into the lightness of dance.

Perhaps that is why the sangeet exists—as therapy for the soul. Weddings can be overwhelming; emotions run high, responsibilities press heavy and change stirs anxieties. Music and dance become the release. They remind us that while marriage is a duty, it is also a festival. While it binds, it also frees.

As I looked back at the dance floor, I smiled. This balance is so very Indian—sacred vows on one side, uninhibited play on the other. Duty and joy. Karma and Leela. The sangeet is that bridge where families discover that before walking together into a lifetime of responsibility, they must first learn how to laugh and dance together.

The first act was Rukmini Dadi's. Draped in shocking-pink silk and armed with her walking stick, she marched up to the choreographer with regal authority.

'Dadi, it's a group dance …' he stammered.

'Group, shmoup! I'm the showstopper of this family. I deserve my own slot!'

Everyone whooped and clapped. And sure enough, when Dadi's number came, she shuffled onto the stage with her dupatta in one hand and her walking stick in the other. Her expressions were so exaggerated they could have revived black-and-white cinema. She ended her performance with a wink and a thumka that left the crowd in stitches. Rohan chuckled under his breath, '*Bas ab, warna stage gir jaayega* [That's enough now, or the stage will collapse],' sending the front row into a fresh round of laughter.

Then it was Ved and Gaurav's turn—the much-hyped 'Gen Z vs Retro' showdown. Ved, dripping in swagger, picked a hip-hop track, spinning and flicking his hands with sharp precision. Gaurav countered with an old-school Bollywood-style performance—arms flailing, eyebrows dancing, hips swaying with unabashed flair and energy. The elders whistled and clapped louder for Gaurav, which made Ved throw up his hands in mock defeat.

'*Sab biased hain* [They're all biased]!' he shouted, pretending to sulk.

The atmosphere was electric. The sangeet had officially found its rhythm.

In the middle of all the noise and the glittering lights, I caught Sanjana slipping quietly out of the hall—just as many of the guests had done that evening, stepping away from the heat and the pounding music for a breath of fresh air.

She was gone only for a short while, but when she returned, there was something faintly different about her. She had on a ready smile for the crowd, yet her eyes carried a trace of unease—as though she had left the noise behind but brought another worry back in with her.

Almost on cue, the next act began—a group took over the stage with infectious Bollywood energy. Their moves were bold and theatrical, drawing loud cheers from the audience. Among the performers was Karan. To everyone else, he was just another guest blending into the evening, his presence unremarkable. But for Sanjana, it was different—she hadn't expected him at her wedding at all, and certainly not performing at the sangeet.

At first, Karan was in the thick of it, matching his group step for step, his charisma drawing whistles and applause. Midway through, the group leapt down from the platform, circling Rohan and Sanjana playfully and pulling them into the spotlight.

The hall erupted with applause and laughter as the couple swayed together in the centre, framed by lights and music. From a distance, it was the perfect sangeet tableau—the radiant couple, the families united in celebration. Yet, up-close, the details told another story. I noticed a stillness in Rohan's eyes—the kind that passed unnoticed in the noise.

Sanjana's smile, though bright, wavered at the edges. Her fingers clutched her dupatta just a little too tightly, betraying the nerves she had tried so carefully to conceal, but could not quite hide.

The night blazed on in a whirl of music and colour.

The sangeet performances closed to thunderous applause, the air still echoing with song. Yet what lingers longest after the music is not always the sound but the silence—the silence where unspoken stories wait their turn to be told.

That is the paradox of relationships. Like a sangeet performance, they may appear effortless to those watching—graceful moves, timed smiles, rehearsed harmony. But on the inside, every step carries its own weight. Some steps are steady, some falter. Some flow rhythmically, others stumble. And yet, together, they still create something the world calls beautiful.

....

THINGS TO THINK ABOUT ...

STORMS VS HARBOURS IN LOVE: Some relationships dazzle like storms but leave us breathless. Others ground us like harbours and bring us peace. True love lies not in fireworks that vanish but in the steadiness that remains.

SHADOWS SHRINK IN THE LIGHT: Concealment magnifies fear. Honesty and open communication may feel uncomfortable, but they strengthen relationships. Real love is not afraid of the truth—it deepens through it.

PAST MEMORIES CAN UNSETTLE THE PRESENT: Old relationships, traumas or unresolved hurts can re-enter our lives unexpectedly. They may not bring love back, but they bring back memories—and unless addressed with honesty, they can cast shadows on the present.

FOUNDATIONS OVER FACADES: Like a building, relationships can look magnificent on the outside, but they will collapse if the foundation is weak. With a strong foundation, even cracks can be repaired, and love can grow stronger after life's tremors.

RELATIONSHIPS NEED MORE THAN JUST CHEMISTRY: The sparkle of attraction and harmony seen from the outside is not enough. The real foundation of lasting bonds is built on trust, respect, communication, shared values and commitment.

THE GHOSTS OF THE PAST: Sometimes we think we've moved on, yet by replaying the pain of old wounds in our minds, we keep vibrating at the frequency of that pain—unconsciously attracting the same patterns back into our lives.

HEALING PATTERNS REQUIRES INNER WORK (THE A-R-I-S-E MODEL): To rise above repetitive relationship struggles, we must:
- A – **Awareness:** Notice recurring patterns.
- R – **Release and Heal:** Let go of old pain instead of recycling it.
- I – **Install New Scripts:** Replace limiting beliefs with affirmations of self-worth and respect.
- S – **Set Boundaries:** Allow in only what nourishes us.
- E – **Energy Shift:** Change within so that we attract and sustain healthier dynamics.

THE DANCE OF RELATIONSHIPS: Like a sangeet performance, relationships demand rhythm, coordination and adjustment. Some steps falter, some flow. What matters is the willingness to recover mid-step and continue together.

•••••••••••••••

The exercises related to the concepts mentioned in this chapter can be found on p. 271.

7

THE ONE-HANDED MONK

The Life-Changing Magic of Real Communication

~

Truth doesn't hide in silence, it waits in
conversation. Shadows shrink not by suspicion
but by the light of honest words.

I had slipped away from the hall around half past ten even though the revelry carried well into midnight. My corner of the palace had grown quiet, save for the faint hum of the ceiling fan and the occasional cry of a peacock somewhere in the gardens. It didn't take me long to fall asleep—it's one of the few perks of monk life: when the body says rest, the mind rarely argues.

And then I heard a knock at my door. Soft at first, hesitant, as if weighing whether to disturb me. Then firmer, edged with urgency. For a split second, half-asleep in that vast old palace, I wondered if it was a ghost trying to scare a monk. I looked at the clock—half past two. My morning perhaps, but for many, still night.

I opened the door to find Rohan standing outside. His shirt was crumpled, his hair tousled and his eyes red-rimmed and heavy. He looked like someone who couldn't sleep.

'Can I ... come in?' he whispered. 'Sorry if I am disturbing you, but I didn't know what else to do.'

I gestured him inside. Before I could even say anything, he began pacing the room like a caged animal. His fingers kept tugging at his hair, rubbing his face, gripping the back of his neck—as though physical touch might anchor him to something real.

'Everything's messed up,' he blurted out, his voice hoarse. 'I thought yesterday was supposed to be ... perfect. And instead—' He stopped, swallowing hard. 'Instead, I feel like I've been played.'

He dropped onto the sofa, elbows pressed into his knees, staring at the marble floor as though it might reveal some answers.

'I don't even know where to begin,' he muttered.

I didn't press.

After a long pause, he lifted his head, his jaw clenched. 'I saw them last night. I heard them actually. Sanjana and Karan. In one of the side gardens, when the sangeet was going on.'

He ran both hands over his face, his voice catching between sentences. 'I wasn't looking for it—trust me. I hate that spying stuff. I had stepped out to take an urgent work call. And that's when ... I heard them. I couldn't catch every word, but their voices ... the words I heard cut deeper than the sharpest knife.'

His words came in bursts—like waves that crash and then retreat, only to rise again stronger.

'She didn't see me. They didn't know I was there. But I know what I saw. I know what I felt. There was a familiarity there ... and it was more than friendship.'

His voice cracked. 'I feel cheated. I feel ... small. Like I've been living in a beautiful dream while the ground underneath was hollow all along. Do you know what it's like to love someone and suddenly wonder if you're just a stand-in? A substitute?'

He turned to me, eyes blazing with hurt, then looked away quickly, ashamed of the tears gathering in them.

'I trusted her with everything. My heart, my life, my ... my very sense of home. And now I can't stop thinking—has she been in love with him all along? Am I just the one she settled for?'

His words spilled out like both a confession and a plea—searching for clarity, aching for release, stuck between suspicion and the desperate hope that he was wrong.

'You trust someone with your soul,' he said, his voice lower now, 'and then you realize they're not who you thought they were. It ... it breaks you.'

The room felt heavy with his anguish. I stayed quiet, letting him empty himself before I could offer a perspective.

Finally, he looked at me, his gaze hollow. 'Tell me, what do I do with this? With what I saw, what I felt? Do I confront her? Do I walk away? Or do I pretend it never happened?'

His voice trembled. 'Tell me how to deal with this pain. It's eating me alive. It wasn't even a long conversation,' he said, almost to himself. 'But sometimes a few sentences are enough to tear you apart.'

He shot back up, pacing the room again, his shadow moving across the walls like a restless ghost.

'I don't know what to believe any more,' he muttered. 'Was it harmless nostalgia? Or is it ... something more? And if it is, then what am I? A fool? A placeholder? Just the man she chose when she couldn't have the one she wanted?'

Finally, he collapsed onto the sofa, burying his face in his hands. This time the tears came—ragged, uncontrolled. His shoulders shook, his breath broke in uneven sobs. For a long moment, the only sound in the room was the muffled strain of his crying, betrayal pressing against the silence heavily.

I sat quietly, letting his emotions settle. Then, without a word, I reached for the jug of water on the side table and poured him a glass. I placed it gently on the table near him, along with a box of tissues. Small gestures, but sometimes they can be the grammar of support.

When he finally looked up, his face was streaked with tears, his eyes glistening with as much exhaustion as pain.

'I feel like my whole world has been ripped open by a conversation that lasted no more than three minutes,' he whispered. 'And I don't know how to restore it.'

I let him sit with his tears a little longer. There is a sacredness to pain when it finally comes out—you don't rush to silence it; instead, you allow space for it to spread and thin out.

'Rohan,' I said gently, 'you are not wrong to feel what you feel. Betrayal, whether real or imagined, doesn't just wound the heart, it shakes the ground beneath. And when the ground feels unsteady, every step feels unsafe.'

He stared at me, breathing unevenly, waiting.

I continued in a steady voice, 'But here is something I've learned—pain always feels permanent in the moment. It feels like your whole world has ended. But pain is not the world, it is like the weather. It comes, it pours, it drenches … And then, if you let it, it passes. The question is not how to escape it, but how to stand through it until the sky clears.'

He swallowed, still trembling, but he held my gaze.

'You heard Sanjana and Karan,' I continued. 'And yes, those voices wounded you in ways you never expected. But remember—what you have right now is not the whole truth, it's only a fragment. A sliver of a story without its context. And fragments can cut sharply, but they are never the full picture. If you build your decisions only on the basis of fragments, it's like building on broken glass—painful, fragile and prone to collapse.'

I paused, letting the words sink in. 'So before you decide whether you've been cheated on or are just a substitute, ask yourself this: Do I want to live in fragments … or do I want to hear the whole story?'

Rohan's chest rose and fell with uneven breaths.

I leaned forward. 'Now, what should you do? Three things. First, don't bottle this up. Speak to Sanjana. Not in an accusatory manner, but with honesty. Hiding your hurt will only make the shadows grow larger. Second, listen to her fully—without interrupting, without letting fear fill the gaps. Give her the dignity of explaining what those three minutes meant to her. And third, once you know the truth, choose— not from fear or anger, but from clarity. Love cannot survive on suspicion, and suspicion cannot survive in the light of truth.'

I paused, then added more softly, 'After her friend introduced Karan to all of you, Sanjana came by and opened her heart to me. Do you know what she told me? She said, fires like Karan burn bright, lighting up everything for a while, and then they're gone. She chose *you*—not because you happened to be there, but because you were the one who gave her peace. Fireworks may light up the sky for a moment, but it is the steady flame that warms a home. And just as I told her then, I tell you now—do not let a passing spark shake a beautiful home, especially when it stands on the strong foundation of trust.'

I let the words rest between us before continuing, 'And trust, Rohan, is built by choosing understanding over misunderstanding ... by choosing communication over assumption.'

For a long moment, Rohan just sat there. His frame softened, as though a quiet knot inside him had finally started to unwind. His lips parted and he whispered, 'Peace ... yes. That's what I felt with her.'

The words seemed to surprise even him. He rubbed his eyes roughly, exhaling a shaky breath, and this time, when the tears came, they carried something gentler, like the beginning of release.

I poured him another glass of water and slid it towards him without a word. He took it, nodding faintly, as if acknowledging both the gesture and the truth he had just uncovered within himself.

For the first time that night, Rohan's face softened. His eyes, still moist, carried not just pain but the faintest trace of calm.

They say trust is like chocolate. Once it sets and breaks, you can try melting and reshaping it—but it never quite returns to the same mould. Is that really true? Maybe. But perhaps the deeper truth is this: Trust isn't meant to be brittle like chocolate at all—it's meant to be like dough. If it dries out, it cracks. But if you knead it, work with it, keep it moist with care, it remains pliable, flexible and can rise again.

Misunderstandings happen all the time. Assumptions are made. And we, in our infinite human wisdom, often sprint to conclusions faster than Usain Bolt on his best day. The question is: Should we jump to conclusions without communication? Without hearing the complete story? Without giving someone the benefit of the doubt? Should we take what we saw—or half-heard—and crown it as reality?

One of the stories I once shared went viral on the internet (now don't ask me how a monk goes viral—I suppose wisdom can be marketed better than me). Stories often touch something close to the heart and strike a deeper chord.

Here's the story:

A little boy named Arnav was asked by his math teacher in school, 'If I give you two mangoes and then another two mangoes, how many will you have?'

'Five,' Arnav replied.

The teacher frowned and repeated the question, this time holding up two fingers on one hand and two on the other. 'Now tell me. Two plus two mangoes?'

Arnav said confidently, 'Five.'

Thinking that the example was perhaps the problem, the teacher switched fruits. 'Okay, now, if I give you two strawberries and then two more strawberries, how many will they be?'

'Four,' said Arnav.

'And two apples plus two apples?'

'Four,' he said again.

The teacher, now relieved that her strategy had worked, went back to the mangoes. 'So tell me, two mangoes and two mangoes make?'

'Five,' said Arnav firmly.

Exasperated, the teacher snapped, 'If two plus two strawberries equals four, and two plus two apples equals four, then how can two plus two mangoes equal five?'

Arnav calmly reached into his school bag, pulled out a mango his mother had packed for lunch, held it up and said, 'Because I already have one.'

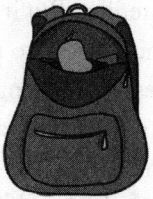

Now, was the teacher wrong? Not at all. Two plus two mangoes *is* four. Was Arnav wrong? Not at all. Two plus two plus one *is* five. Both were right, but they had different perspectives.

And that, my friends, is how assumptions work. We don't ask. We don't check. We don't want to know the whole picture. And the other side doesn't clarify, doesn't express, doesn't explain—until asked. The result? Two truths colliding, neither wrong, but both incomplete.

Whether in relationships or at work, the principle is the same. Before jumping to a conclusion, ask questions. And when needed, express yourself. Clarify. Communicate. Don't leave your hidden mango lying quietly in the bag while someone else is busy calculating two plus two.

Sanjana, in our story, was going to share her hidden mango with Rohan. But before she could, Rohan put two and two together—and we all know what number he landed on.

Trust is built on open communication. Not on the absence of problems, but on the willingness to talk through them. Think of any strong bond—marriage, friendship, even professional partnerships—a third person doesn't ruin them. What ruins them is when one entertains that third person, or when suspicion about that third person festers without open and honest conversation.

Yes, honest communication can be uncomfortable. It can feel awkward, even threatening. But it is the very basis of trust. It's what turns brittle chocolate into pliable dough. It's what ensures that when life tests the strength of the walls—and it will—the house doesn't collapse, because the foundation has been reinforced again and again.

So the next time you find yourself jumping to conclusions, please pause. Ask. Share. And remember: Somewhere, in every relationship, there's always a hidden mango waiting to be revealed.

My guru, Radhanath Swami, has been taking us on pilgrimages—yatras—to holy places for over three decades now. What began as small groups of barely ten eager pilgrims has today swelled to congregations of over ten thousand. Imagine the logistics: buses rolling across dusty roads, kitchens that would impress National Geographic, volunteers chopping vegetables like soldiers in formation, the daily rhythm of visiting sacred sites and evenings filled with kirtan and talks. One can only imagine the management it requires—sometimes it feels like we are organizing the world's largest destination wedding.

On one such yatra, a monk friend of mine, who had only recently joined the ashram, was travelling on a bus. He was sitting next to a man he didn't know. The elderly man, draped in a shawl, was softly chanting his japa—the meditative repetition of God's names using prayer beads, which are kept inside a small cloth bag called a bead bag. Traditionally, one chants with the right hand, keeping the left free. But my monk friend noticed that this man was using his left hand.

Now, the enthusiasm of a new monk is a dangerous thing. My friend was eager to correct what he thought was a glaring mistake. How can this senior devotee not know the basics, he thought to himself. But he also had the decency to wait. He decided to let the man finish this round of chanting. So he watched. And he waited.

Minutes passed. The bus rocked gently on the bumpy road. The chanting went on steadily. My monk friend, cradled by the motion of the bus, dozed off. When he woke up after a sudden jolt—the bus had jumped over a pothole—he turned groggily to his neighbour, who was still chanting peacefully, his eyes closed. But the shawl had slipped from the man's shoulder.

My friend's heart sank. The man didn't have a right hand.

In that instant, the young monk felt three things at once. He felt shock, because his assumption was so off the mark; shame, because he had judged without knowing the whole story; and gratitude, because sleep had saved him from embarrassing himself, and hurting the heart of someone who was quietly carrying both his loss and his devotion with dignity.

Now, let's talk about the word 'assume'. Break it down and what do you get? Ass – U – Me. Yes, you've probably heard this joke before. Because when we assume without clarifying, we make an ass out of you and me.

None of us is an ass—nor is Rohan. He's a gentleman. His assumption was born not from arrogance but from attachment, from love, from the fear of losing Sanjana. Most of us are coming from a good place when we make assumptions. We're just not always doing it the right way. And doing things right, in relationships, means one thing: open, clear communication.

So how do we communicate in such moments?

- **Pause before You Pounce**

  In relationships, our first instinct is often to confront, accuse or collapse. But wisdom begins with pausing. The pause gives space for emotions to settle and for facts to surface.

- **Replace 'Why Did You?' with 'Can You Help Me Understand?'**

  'Why did you do this?' sounds like courtroom cross-examination. But 'Can you help me understand what happened?' is an invitation to honesty. The first triggers defensiveness, the second encourages dialogue.

- **Facts First, Feelings Second**

  Lead with what you saw or heard, not with your interpretation. 'I saw you speaking with him in the garden' is a fact. 'You must still love him' is an interpretation. Confusing the two leads to fireworks, not building a strong foundation.

- **Assume Good Intent, Until Proven Otherwise**

  Most people don't wake up thinking, How can I ruin my partner's life today? Our loved ones are usually trying, even if imperfectly. Giving them the benefit of the doubt is not naive, it's courageous.

- **Express before It Festers**

  Hidden mangoes (to borrow from Arnav's story) don't rot because they exist—they rot because they're not revealed. Communication is the act of placing the mango on the table before someone miscalculates two plus two.

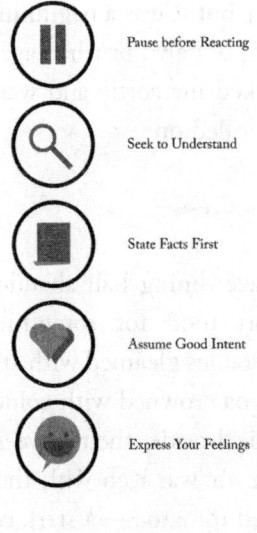

- Pause before Reacting
- Seek to Understand
- State Facts First
- Assume Good Intent
- Express Your Feelings

~

I looked back at Rohan, who had now grown quiet.

'Rohan,' I said softly, 'none of us is immune to assumptions. Misunderstandings will happen but the point is to not stop at that stage. We must try to move beyond fragments and choose clarity over imagination.'

He nodded slowly, a small ripple of relief moving through him. His breathing was steady even though his eyes still carried the echo of turmoil.

'You love Sanjana,' I continued, 'and that is why this hurts so much. But don't let that love be swallowed by silence or suspicion. Speak. Share. Ask. The very things you fear saying aloud are the things that, when expressed, can set you free.'

Rohan pressed his palms together, not in prayer but in exhaustion. His lips parted and he said in a quiet voice, 'I'll try.'

It wasn't a declaration, but it was a beginning.

Outside, the faint hint of dawn brushed against the night sky as Rohan rose, thanked me softly and went to snatch a little rest before the day rolled on.

∽

That afternoon, the palace dining hall abandoned its usual trays of Indian comfort food for something altogether different—Italian. Long tables gleamed with steaming bowls of pasta, piping hot lasagna crowned with golden cheese and baskets of warm focaccia breads, their olive-studded crust glistening invitingly. The air was rich with the fragrance of basil, oregano and roasted tomatoes—a stark contrast to the lingering aroma of the previous night's dal baati churma, which still hung faintly in the palace corridors.

Ved and Gaurav had claimed the centre table, already turning lunch into a performance. Their exchanges were light and playful on the surface, yet beneath that something unspoken was forming—the first fragile threads of a bond that neither had given a name to yet. In time, it would grow into something far deeper.

Ved, with all the confidence of the Gen Z, twirled his fork, neatly catching the spaghetti in one smooth motion—like a native of some quaint Italian town rather than a boy from Mumbai.

Gaurav, on the other hand, was battling with his plate. The spaghetti slid off his fork like a stubborn child refusing to be picked up. After a few failed attempts, he finally stabbed the pasta straight through, lifted it and said, 'Arré, bhai, this is impossible! By the time I catch it, half of it escapes. Indian food is straightforward—one roti, one bite. Simple.'

Ved raised his fork with a flourish, a perfect coil of spaghetti dangling proudly. 'See? Technique. This is why Gen Z survives anywhere—Italy, India or Instagram.'

Everyone around burst into laughter. Gaurav, refusing to concede, piled more pasta onto his plate and said with mock seriousness, 'Don't worry. From Rome to Rajasthan, they'll clap for me too. It's called cultural exchange.'

As the laughter continued, a stray strand of spaghetti landed on Gaurav's kurta, leaving a tomato-red stain. Ved pounced on the moment. '*Bas!* This is why I keep saying tomato sauce should be banned at weddings. The haldi ceremony this evening will create enough stains—do we really need to add tomato sauce to the mix?'

The table erupted again, forks pausing mid-air as the playful duel between the two became the real entertainment of the afternoon.

Just then, Priya entered, carrying her plate. She paused, her eyes drawn to the scene—Gaurav's calm humour balancing Ved's melodrama. She couldn't help but smile.

Taking a seat nearby, she teased, 'Gauravji, I hope you weren't planning to wear this kurta again tonight. The way it's been collecting stains, the laundry man will need divine intervention to properly clean it.'

Gaurav dabbed at his kurta with a napkin and said, 'Don't worry, Priyaji, I've decided to auction off this kurta after the wedding. Object: *Abstract Art in Tomato Sauce.*'

Everyone laughed, Gaurav grinned sheepishly and Ved clapped his hands in mock jubilance. Priya noticed the steadiness in Gaurav's response—how he could laugh at himself without a flicker of defensiveness. It was a small thing, easily missed by others.

She had also begun to notice more about him over the past couple of days—that Gaurav was the kind of man who was naturally kind, quietly helpful, supportive without making a show of it and always carrying an easy energy that lifted the room. Watching him with Ved now, she could see how well the two had begun to flow together, their banter laced with both humour and warmth.

Just then, Rakesh spotted her. 'Priya! Why are you sitting all the way there?' he called out. 'Why share your company only with them? Come join us, we'd love some fun here too!'

She hesitated, though only for a moment, before moving towards our table. Rakesh, Lakshmi and I had been sharing stories over lunch—about the food and about the chaos of managing families at weddings.

As Priya settled down beside us, Rakesh beamed. 'Good, now the scene is complete. One side of the hall is full of noise, the other side with wisdom. The balance has been restored.'

We all laughed. For a while, the air felt lighter, the conversation flowing as smoothly as the tiramisu served that afternoon.

Rakesh leaned forward, serving Priya a spoonful of lasagna before she could stop him. 'You should try this, beta. Not too heavy, not too oily—Italian food is ... sophisticated.' He smiled warmly, almost awkwardly, like a man trying to remember how to be gentle.

Priya managed a polite smile, but it didn't stay for long. Her fork paused midway. Her eyes clouded, and then, almost without meaning to, she turned to me. 'Swamiji,' she said softly, 'tell me something honestly. Can years of neglect be made up with a few smiles? With a spoon of lasagna?'

The words fell into the space between her and Rakesh like stones into a pond. Lakshmi shifted uncomfortably, and even I felt the weight of her unspoken ache.

'Priya ...' Rakesh began, his voice faltering. 'It's not like that.'

Her lips curled into a trembling smile, one that didn't reach her eyes. 'Then what *is* it like, Papa? People saw your light—your generosity, your grace, your strength. But I saw what they didn't ... the distance, the silence. Why? Because I wasn't good enough? Not fair enough? Not sharp enough? Or simply ... not worthy enough?'

Her voice cracked, but she didn't stop. 'I grew up thinking I was unworthy of your love. And now, suddenly, you pass me the lasagna and expect me to believe something else?'

The table went silent. Rakesh's fingers tightened around his napkin, his knuckles pale. He looked down, then up at Priya, then away again—like a man trapped in a cage of his own making.

'Beta ...' he whispered. 'Please don't think that.'

'Then tell me. Tell me, what should I think?' Priya pressed, her voice sharper now. 'Tell me what it really was. Because I've lived my whole life believing I was invisible to you. And unless you tell me otherwise, that's all I know.'

Rakesh exhaled slowly, his eyes wet, his jaw clenched. He looked at me for a moment, as if silently asking whether to keep carrying the burden or to finally lay it down. I gave him the faintest nod.

He turned back to Priya. 'You think I didn't love you?' His voice shook. 'Priya, you are my heartbeat. More precious to me than my own life. A father's heart ... it often belongs most to his daughter. But I—' He looked away, as if the words were too heavy to say aloud.

Priya's eyes glistened. 'Then why, Papa? Why did you make me feel unloved all these years?'

Rakesh gripped the edge of the table. His shoulders heaved as he whispered, 'Because I thought if I showed you my love, I might lose you.'

Priya froze, confused. 'Lose me?'

Rakesh closed his eyes for a moment, gathering strength. 'When you were very young, a close friend dragged me to a renowned astrologer. I didn't believe in such things, but I went anyway. That man ... he told me your stars showed that calamity would befall you—a danger to your life—if you received too much attention from me before the age of forty. His words haunted me. I hated them. But I couldn't ignore them.'

Priya gasped, her fork clattering against the plate.

'So I made the hardest decision of my life,' Rakesh said. 'I gave you everything you needed—your schooling, your art, your independence. But I withheld my affection. Because I knew everyone else would give it to you anyway. You are kind, Priya—people gravitate towards you. Everyone loved you. But I thought that if I stepped back, I would still be able to protect you. I believed that by keeping my distance, I was shielding you.'

Priya's chair scraped faintly against the floor as she leaned forward, her eyes shining with a mixture of anger and sorrow. 'Shielding me?' she asked, her voice rising. 'Someone said it, and you did it. Just like that. But what about my childhood, Papa? What about all the years I cried myself to sleep thinking I was unwanted? Do you think that was right?'

The words cut deep. Rakesh opened his mouth but no sound came out. His hand trembled slightly against the tablecloth.

I placed my palm gently on the table. 'Priya,' I said softly, 'can I share something?' She nodded reluctantly, her jaw still tight.

'I understand what you're feeling,' I continued. 'To grow up with a father's presence but not his warmth—that is a wound no child should ever carry. But I also see what Rakeshji is saying. Sometimes life forces us into making impossible choices. There is what the world calls "right", the objective right. And then there is the "right" that exists only in our small worlds, where love and fear collide. For your father, you were his world. Whether that astrologer was right or wrong wasn't the point. The only thing he was concerned about was that if there was even the slightest chance of losing you, he couldn't take it. So he chose distance, thinking it was protection.'

Priya's tears spilled over, her voice trembling as she cut in, 'But does astrology even make sense, Swamiji? Should anyone's life be shaped by it? I lost years because of this!'

I nodded. 'You're right to ask that. Astrology has been called a science, but not the kind that dictates fate with certainty. It's more analytical—a way of observing tendencies, strengths, weaknesses, opportunities and threats. A kind of ancient SWOT analysis of life. But even then, it is like Google Maps—it can show you the different available routes, but it cannot drive the car for you. Some experts may be able to predict with uncanny accuracy, others may not. It is not perfect.'

Priya shook her head, unconvinced. 'So what then? Should we gamble away our lives because of it?'

I replied, 'No. What we *should* do is understand that each situation is unique. Some parents, upon hearing such a prediction, might dismiss it. Others, like your father, might act on it out of fear and love. Was doing this right or wrong? In black-and-white terms, maybe it was wrong. But if you're looking through the lens of love, it was the only choice he thought he had. And that's what makes this so complicated. Right and wrong aren't always clearly defined. Sometimes they are just two difficult paths, and we choose the one we hope hurts less.'

Priya's shoulders slumped, her tears flowing freely now.

I looked at her gently. 'Your father's silence wasn't the absence of love. It was a clumsy, painful manifestation of it. A love so strong that he chose to appear cruel, if it meant that would keep you safe. That doesn't make your pain any less valid, Priya. It just shows that behind the hurt, you were always loved.'

Rakesh's eyes welled over as he looked at her. 'I did it out of love, beta. I would rather have you hate me than risk losing you. And yet, in doing so ... I broke your heart. And mine too along with it.'

Priya sat frozen. 'Papa ...' Her voice broke into a whisper. 'All these years ... all these years I thought I was less. And you let me believe it.'

Rakesh's face crumpled. 'Because I thought silence was safer than the truth. Forgive me, Priya. Please forgive me.'

Her sobs broke through the last of the distance between them. She reached for him, clutching his hand. He drew her into his arms, holding her tightly, his strong frame trembling as decades of unspoken love poured out at last. Lakshmi watched the scene with tears flowing down her face.

I let the silence linger, then spoke softly. 'Sometimes the cruellest wounds don't come from a lack of love but from a love kept hidden. Astrology may or may not be true—but a father's heart is. And Priya, your father's love was never absent. Only hidden. Unseen, but always there.'

Priya wept into her father's shoulder. Rakesh stroked her hair, whispering, 'My daughter ... my light ... forgive me.'

Around us, lunch went on. Laughter, chatter, the clinking of plates. But at our table, a ceremony had already taken place—not with turmeric or flowers, but with truth, tears and a father's love finally set free.

∼

This was yet another story of misunderstandings, assumptions and a silence that had lasted too long. Most of the time, we think of a lack of communication as a kind of weakness. But in Rakesh's case, the silence was not born of carelessness. It was against the will. It was not neglect, it was desperation. And that's where the story becomes more complex, more human.

In our scriptures, there is the story of Kunti and Karna. Kunti was only a young girl when, through a divine boon, she was gifted with Karna. She was barely seven. She did not know what to do with such a blessing, or such a burden. Out of fear and helplessness, she placed him in a basket and set him afloat, praying that destiny would be kinder than her circumstances. Years later, when Karna grew into a warrior unmatched, she still kept the truth—that he was her son—locked within her. It was not her fault; she had no choice. Was she right? Was she wrong? When she finally revealed the truth, it was on the eve of the great war, when Karna had already pledged his loyalty to Duryodhana, his friend. It was too late by then—love and duty stood on opposite sides of the battlefield.

Friends, that's the point. Yes, there are objective rights and wrongs. When someone commits a crime—theft, violence, abuse—there is no debate needed. But there is also another space, a grey space beyond right and wrong, where life is less about judgement and more about empathy. A space where people make choices not because they are selfish or careless, but because they are helpless.

Often, those choices come with collateral damage. The wound may run deep, sometimes beyond repair. Priya's pain was real. Her father's silence cut her childhood up in ways he never intended. And yet, for Rakesh, his silence was not absence but his way—however flawed—of protecting her.

Am I suggesting that such things should happen? That parents should withhold love in the name of protection? No. Am I excusing the hurt? No. But what I am saying is this: Life is not black and white. It is complicated, layered, nuanced.

And in your own life, dear reader, you will face this too. People will do things that hurt you. You may do things that hurt others. Before rushing to make assumptions, before letting judgement take over, pause. Look for the hidden mango. Ask yourself, Is there a truth I haven't seen yet? Is there a pain behind the silence?

This doesn't mean every act is justified. It doesn't mean every choice was wise. But to live with empathy is to see beyond the obvious—to say sorry when it is needed and to forgive when required. None of these are easy to do. But even a small step in that direction makes life gentler, lighter, more liveable.

Would Priya be able to forgive her father? Would he be able to forgive himself? Would they be able to heal? I do not know. But one thing is certain—their journey had begun. The journey of a love unsaid, now finding its voice.

•••••••••••••••

THINGS TO THINK ABOUT ...

ESCAPE PAIN OR ALLOW IT TO PASS: Pain always feels permanent in the moment. It feels like our whole world has ended. Pain convinces us it will last forever. It fills every corner of our world until we forget what light feels like. But pain isn't the world—it's a passing season. It storms, it cools down and then, quietly, it begins to fade.

FRAGMENTS VS THE FULL STORY: Making decisions based on fragments of information is like building on broken glass—fragile and painful. What we hear or see may be partly true, but it is rarely the whole picture.

THE DANGER OF ASSUMPTIONS: Half-heard words, incomplete stories and silence can feel sharper than lies. Assumptions often hurt more than the truth because they replace curiosity with judgement.

THE HIDDEN-MANGO PRINCIPLE: Like the boy who had an extra mango in his bag, both sides in a relationship may hold unseen truths. Misunderstandings arise when one doesn't reveal and the other doesn't ask. Trust requires both—expression and inquiry.

THE ART OF COMMUNICATION:
- Pause before reacting—let emotions settle.
- Replace accusation ('Why did you …') with curiosity ('Help me understand …').
- State the facts before giving interpretations.
- Assume good intent until proven otherwise.
- Express hurt before it festers.

BEYOND RIGHT AND WRONG: Not every silence is neglect. Sometimes it is helplessness, fear or love expressed clumsily. Empathy allows us to see the story behind the choices, even if they hurt. There are moments when distinguishing between right and wrong is not easy, and all we can do is choose the path that lets us breathe a little easier.

••••••••••••••••

The exercises related to the concepts mentioned in this chapter can be found on p. 273.

8

SACRED HALDI
The Power of Vulnerability

Life is not about carrying everything on our own shoulders. It's about knowing when to put our guards down, when to ask for a hand and when to let our heart speak the truth it has hidden for too long.

After the indulgent Italian lunch, the palace seemed to exhale and settle into a gentler rhythm. The long dining hall gradually emptied as families drifted off to their own spaces. The afternoon sun poured through the arched windows, casting lazy golden patches across the marble floor, inviting everyone to slow down.

In the courtyard, the decorators were already at work for the haldi. Brass bowls of turmeric paste were being arranged on low wooden tables surrounded by marigold garlands and banana leaves. Attendants tested the placement of cushions, fussed over floral rangolis and debated whether the yellow drapes should spill across the arches or be tied neatly into bunches. The faint beat of a dholak drifted in from somewhere, its rhythm playful, almost teasing—a promise of what was to come. The entire palace seemed to be suspended between two moods—the languor of the afternoon and the anticipation of celebration.

The haldi ceremony is one of the most playful yet profound rituals of an Indian wedding. At first glance, it seems simple—family and friends smear turmeric paste on the bride and groom, laughter flowing as everyone joins in. But the joyous celebrations are backed by ancient wisdom.

In Indian culture, turmeric is not just a spice. It is sacred. Its golden hue symbolizes purity, protection and auspicious beginnings. It is believed to cleanse the body of toxins, guard against negativity and bless the couple with both radiance and resilience. The glow it leaves is more than just physical, it is a spiritual reminder that marriage is not merely about two people coming together but about preparing their minds, hearts and souls for vows that carry the weight of a lifetime's promise.

The ritual is playful on the surface the surface—songs, teasing and laughter, turmeric flying in every direction—but within all this rests a deeper message: Before you step into a sacred bond, cleanse what must not be carried forward. Just as turmeric clears blemishes, forgiveness clears the stains of the heart. Just as haldi shields the skin, kindness shields love from bitterness.

In many ways, isn't that what life and relationships constantly ask of us? To pause, to wipe away the dust of assumptions, to heal the marks left by silence, to prepare ourselves again and again for new beginnings?

For the couple, the haldi is about entering marriage glowing, both inside and out. For the rest of us, it is a gentle reminder that relationships too need their haldi moments—moments of cleansing, healing and blessing.

~

That afternoon, I found myself sitting on the cool stone steps of one of the palace halls—a tucked-away corner from where one could watch the bustle without being caught in it. A book rested in my hands, but I was reading the silence more than the pages.

It was there that Ved found me, his sneakers squeaking faintly on the marble, phone in hand, sunglasses perched unnecessarily on his head since the sun was already mellowing.

'Gaurji!' Ved grinned. 'This is such a postcard moment. You, ancient palace, ancient wisdom ... and then me, the Wi-Fi password hunter. Total contrast.'

I looked up from my book. 'And which category do you fall into—art exhibit in the ancient palace or palace nuisance?'

Ved plopped down beside me on the step, stretching his legs out like he owned the place. 'Depends on who you ask,' he said. 'Nani thinks I'm the reincarnation of Picasso. Mom thinks I'm a full-time debit-card notification. And you …' he said, tilting his head and raising an eyebrow behind his shades, 'I think you're still undecided.'

I smiled, closing the book. 'I'm leaning towards … Picasso on EMI.'

He laughed so loudly that a couple passing by turned their heads. He lowered his voice. 'Seriously, though, you always find these cool corners to hide in. People are running around setting up for the haldi and you're chilling like a Zen influencer.'

'Reading a book isn't hiding,' I said. 'It's just watching the world with subtitles.'

Ved chuckled, but I noticed he didn't pull out his phone immediately. He just sat there, glancing every now and then at the action in the distance—decorators arguing about the marigold placement, some guests rehearsing one more dance step before abandoning it in laughter and the staff carrying bowls of turmeric paste towards the courtyard.

He leaned back on his elbows. 'Tonight's going to be war, you know. The haldi is never just a ceremony—it's a combat sport. I'm telling you, people come dressed in yellow only because they know that by the end they'll look like turmeric pakoras.'

'True,' I said. 'The haldi is the one wedding ritual where the family's mission is not blessings but creating maximum mess.'

He laughed again, shaking his head, the sound echoing lightly across the corridor. 'You monks have it easy. No cousins ambushing you with turmeric, no uncles chasing you with dholaks.'

'True,' I replied with a smile. 'Our ambushes are quieter. We just get attacked with questions.'

Ved grinned, and I caught a fleeting change in his eyes, like a faint crease tugging at the edges of his smile, a ripple beneath the casual ease he carried. It was just a flicker, but it was there, peeking out between the jokes.

He stayed quiet for a beat, tracing circles on the marble step with his finger. Then he said, 'You know, Gaurji ... I really wanted to thank you. For helping Mom and Nanu understand me a little better.'

I tilted my head. 'Understand what?'

'What I want to do in life. My art,' he said, glancing sideways at me. 'They've always thought of it as ... a hobby. Something that looks nice on a wall, but not something serious. Mom wanted me to get into business, or at least something practical. Nanu thinks the same. But when you spoke to them the other day, you explained how art isn't just decoration—it's expression. And ... that meant a lot to me.'

Ved slipped a small sketchbook out of his tote, its corners worn soft, the cover smudged with fingerprints of graphite and charcoal. He flipped it open, hesitated for a second, as if debating whether to share, then angled it towards me.

'Here,' he murmured, 'some of my latest sketches.'

The pages breathed with strokes of charcoal and ink. Faces half-lit, bodies captured as if in mid-motion, a bird straining against the bars of a cage, a boy standing in the rain beneath an umbrella far too small. The drawings weren't polished like gallery pieces. Rather, they were raw, restless, alive. Each sketch carried weight, like his laughter—something unspoken threaded into the lines.

I studied the sketches for a moment, then looked up at him. 'Beautiful. You're right—art isn't just what we see. It's what the artist doesn't say in words.'

He gave a small shrug, feigning nonchalance, but I could tell that he was proud of his work.

Sometimes, the deepest truths are like a frightened cat. If you chase them, they withdraw further into their shell. If you wait with warmth, they come and sit beside you. So I didn't ask. I simply sat, turning the pages of his sketchbook, leaving the silence open for him.

After a while, Ved said gently, 'You know ... some time ago, I was passing by Dadi's suite. The door was slightly open ...'

And with those words, I could almost see what he had seen.

The atmosphere in the corridor was hushed, heavy with the stillness of the afternoon. Ved paused, hearing muffled sobs from inside Dadi's room. His first instinct was to move on—but the familiarity of the voice rooted him to the spot. He slipped behind the curtain by the door, heart beating fast, afraid of being caught and yet unable to walk away. Through the slit, he saw it—Priya, with her head buried in Rukmini Dadi's lap, her shoulders shaking, and Dadi's weathered hand stroking her hair in slow, steady circles.

'Dadi ...' Priya's voice broke. 'It's been so long since Vinay left. Ved was just two. He never knew what it was to be held by his father. And I ... I tried to be everything for him: mother and father, protector and provider. I have you all, yes ... And Ved, he's my joy. My work, my business, they keep me occupied. But Dadi ...' she gasped, her tears spilling harder, 'I've been so lonely.'

Ved's fists clenched behind the curtain. He had never heard his mother sound so hollow, so raw.

Priya pressed her face harder into her grandmother's lap. 'And now ... after meeting Gaurav ... I feel something I thought I'd buried when Vinay died. Gaurav is kind, gentle, funny and caring ... he makes me feel safe again. I've started to like him, Dadi. And that scares me. Because my heart was always Vinay's. Is it betrayal if my heart stirs for someone else?'

Her words cracked open her grief and she dissolved into fresh sobs.

Dadi held her closer, one hand wiping the tears streaking down Priya's cheeks. Her voice, though tender, carried the confidence of one who had seen enough life to understand pain. 'Pagli ... why do you carry guilt like a badge? Do you think your Vinay would want this? He adored your laughter, your spirit. Do you think he's sitting somewhere counting your tears and demanding loyalty in spite of your loneliness? No, Priya. He'd want you to bloom. To live.'

Priya shook her head violently. 'But my soul has only known him. To even feel something for another man ... Dadi, it feels like I'm tearing myself apart.'

At this, Dadi fell silent. Her eyes, for the first time, looked far away—as though searching her own past. The hand stroking Priya's hair slowed. When she spoke again, her voice was steady, but it carried the cracks of memory.

'I understand more than you know. When your dada left, your papa was still so young. And there was a time, beta, when I too felt a flicker of companionship again. Someone who made me feel less alone, less widowed. I was at a crossroads—my duty to my son on one side, my heart's longing on the other. And I chose duty. But don't mistake me—it wasn't easy. The heart, Priya ... the heart has its own stubborn hungers.'

Priya lifted her head slowly, her swollen eyes searching Dadi's face. 'And were you right, Dadi?' she whispered.

Dadi's lips trembled, the hint of a smile showing and then disappearing at once. 'Right? Wrong? Life isn't that neat, child. Some nights, when your Papa was small, and I was exhausted, I'd wonder what it would've been like if I'd chosen differently. But then I'd look at him—my responsibility, my boy—and I knew why I had stayed. We all carry the lives we didn't choose along with the ones we did.'

She cupped Priya's face firmly in her hands. 'So now, it is your turn. I chose duty. What will you choose?'

Priya collapsed again into her lap, trembling, whispering only one word over and over again: 'Dadi ... Dadi ...'

Behind the curtain, Ved felt his throat tighten. He had always seen his mother as strong, untouchable in the face of troubles, the centre of his world. To see her breaking—to hear her yearning for love, confessing guilt and being soothed like a child—it tore something inside him. A son's instinct to protect, to fix, rose in him, but he was powerless, frozen in the shadows. His chest ached, and when he finally slipped away unnoticed, the sound of her sobs still clung to him like the turmeric stains that would not wash away easily.

And just like that, Ved fell silent beside me on the steps, his eyes fixed on his sneakers.

When Priya broke down in Dadi's lap, something extraordinary happened. It was not just a widow sharing her grief or a granddaughter confiding in her grandmother. It was the moment when a carefully guarded heart allowed itself to be *seen*. For years, Priya had built herself up like a fortress—the strong mother, the independent woman, the tireless worker. But here, her walls had finally cracked.

And that's the truth of life, friends—strength is not always about holding up the mask. Sometimes strength lies in allowing the mask to fall, in whispering the words we thought we'd never dare to say aloud: I'm lonely. I'm scared. I still have longings.

Think of it like holding a glass of water. At first the weight feels light—like holding a feather. Hold the glass for a minute, no problem. For thirty minutes, and you start to feel the effort. By the time it's an hour, your arm starts to tremble. And anything longer than that feels unbearable. The weight hasn't changed, your endurance has. The longer you hold on, the heavier it feels. That's what emotional burdens do too. A memory, a guilt, a longing—none of them weigh much in the moment. But if carried constantly, day after day, they begin to gnaw at us and weigh us down. They steal our peace, rob us of joy and, in the worst cases, grow into anxiety, depression or chronic loneliness.

Now imagine the same situation but with two small changes:

- You're allowed to *set the glass down* every now and then. Even if you have to pick it up again later, that brief rest gives your arm relief.
- Or someone comes along and *holds the glass with you* for a while. Instantly, the weight feels lighter—not because the glass has become less heavy, but because you're no longer carrying it alone.

That is the power of vulnerability. Speaking your truth—to a trusted person, or when it feels too sensitive, into a journal, or in prayer—is like putting the glass down. And when someone listens, supports or even shares their own struggles, the burden is divided.

The real challenge, of course, is that we don't want to appear 'weak.' So we camouflage—smiles, busyness, polished answers like, 'I'm fine.' But vulnerability requires honesty and humility: taking off the layers and letting someone glimpse the raw, unfiltered self beneath.

But—and this is important—*who* we're vulnerable with matters. Not every ear deserves your story. Choose wisely—people who are trustworthy, people who wish you well. People who act with wisdom and care, not judgement or gossip.

Now, imagine two patients in a hospital sharing their stories. One has a knee injury, the other has high blood pressure. They encourage each other, laugh about their struggles and feel lighter. But let's be honest, they still need a doctor!

That's vulnerability too—sharing with equals helps you feel seen, but sometimes you need a guide, a mentor or even professional help to heal.

Here's the paradox. We think vulnerability will make us weaker. In truth, it makes us lighter, stronger and freer. Because once you speak about the burden aloud, it stops controlling you in silence. Once you share it, you realize you're not alone.

Priya, in her trembling confession, was not betraying Vinay. She was simply laying down her glass of water for a moment, letting someone else support its weight. And in that act, she wasn't breaking—she was beginning to heal.

And yes, life does not always place in front of us choices that are clear-cut and simple. Often, the hardest decisions are not between good and bad, right and wrong, virtue and vice. Those are easy to judge. The true struggle comes when life places before us two rights that cannot coexist.

On one side stands responsibility—the commitments we carry towards family, children, parents, society. On the other side stands the longing of the heart—the quiet ache for love, companionship and fulfilment. One side is shaped by expectations and roles that keep life steady. The other is stirred by a yearning for colour, connection and meaning, but is sometimes shadowed with guilt or doubt.

And then the question rises, quietly but mercilessly: What am I supposed to choose?

The truth, dear reader, is that there is no perfect choice. Every choice comes with its own price.

Rukmini Dadi chose duty, and lived with the quiet ache of a loneliness she wore like a second skin. Priya longs for companionship, but guilt hovers around her heart like an uninvited guest. One lived with sacrifice, the other wrestles with longing. Neither was fully wrong, neither fully right. Both were simply human.

That is what life teaches us: We are not always choosing between wrong and right. Sometimes we are choosing which wound we can live with.

When life places us at such a crossroads, the wisest step is not to search for a path that pleases everyone—for such a path rarely exists. The wiser question to ask is: Which choice brings me inner peace? Which choice will my conscience allow me to live with?

And sometimes, one's courage is not defined by what we choose—whether it be responsibility or longing—but by the honesty with which we own it. Because honesty, even when uncomfortable, brings dignity. It transforms regret into responsibility. It says: I did not run away from my truth. I faced it. And this is the life I have chosen.

Think of your own life. Have you ever stayed in a job that suffocated you, but you did it anyway to keep your family comfortable? Or perhaps you walked away from someone you loved because the circumstances or responsibility towards your family didn't allow it. Or maybe you stayed in a relationship longer than you should have, because you were afraid of breaking someone's heart. Were you wrong? Or were you simply doing the best you could with what life handed you?

Dear reader, let me say this to you: You are not broken because you struggled to decide. You are not weak because you hesitated. Humanity is messy, layered, complicated—but also magnificent.

So if you stand at a crossroads today, do not make the choice that makes you a hero in someone else's story. Make the choice that allows you to respect yourself when you look in the mirror. And if you already carry the weight of a choice made long ago—forgive yourself. You did not fail. You simply chose one right over another.

Life will not always hand you clarity. But if you walk with empathy—for yourself and for others—even the hardest choices can lead to growth.

And remember, it is not always about choosing the brighter path, but about walking whichever path you choose with truth in your heart. That truth, that honesty is what imparts dignity to the journey.

~

Ved sat quietly, now folding and unfolding the corner of his sketchbook page, his fingers restless. His gaze stayed on the lines he had doodled absent-mindedly, and when he finally spoke, his voice was low, uncertain.

'Gaurji ... what if ...' he said, hesitating. 'What if Mom actually chooses Gaurav Uncle?'

I looked at him gently, letting him continue.

'I don't know how I'm supposed to feel about it. Part of me ...' he said, swallowing, 'feels weird. Because I've only ever thought of him as, you know, some family friend. Always smiling, always around. But if Mom ... if she really likes him ... and he ...' Ved paused. 'What if he becomes my dad?'

He let the word linger awkwardly in the air, as if testing it for the first time.

'I mean, what does that even mean for me? For us?' He laughed suddenly, though thinly. 'I'm nineteen. I'm not a little kid waiting to be adopted. And yet … there's a part of me that wonders. What if I can finally find out what it feels like to have a dad? Not Nanu, not my uncles, not relatives filling in. But someone who's … mine.'

He looked away quickly. 'Sometimes I wonder what it would've been like, you know? To grow up with a father taking me to cricket matches, scolding me for staying out late, teaching me how to shave without cutting half my chin off.' A wry smile appeared on his lips. 'Nanu did what he could, but it's different.'

He drew a long breath, then said, 'I don't know if Gaurav Uncle even wants that … or if I even have the right to want it. But when I see the way he talks to Mom, the way he listens to her, the way he treats me without ever making me feel small … I think … maybe … maybe I could let him in.'

He paused. 'But what if it all goes wrong? What if I let him into my heart, and it doesn't last? I don't think I could handle losing … another dad.'

His words broke off there. He put his sketchbook down, and leaned forward, elbows on his knees.

'Ved,' I said, 'to want a father, to wonder what it would be like to have someone in that role, is absolutely natural.'

His eyes flicked up at me, cautious, searching.

'You've grown up filling that space with your imagination,' I continued. 'Sometimes with questions, sometimes with quiet envy when you saw your friends with their fathers. That longing doesn't go away just because you're older. In fact, when you see love in your proximity—like the way you see your mother smiling with Gaurav—it can stir that longing even more strongly.'

He shifted slightly, folding the edge of the sketchbook again.

I continued, 'But listen, Ved. Fatherhood is not acquired overnight. It is a relationship built step by step. If life takes that turn, Gaurav may one day become more than just your "uncle". But whether he becomes your father—that is not decided by marriage alone. It will depend on how you both choose to walk towards each other.'

Ved's lips pressed into a line, his brow furrowing.

'Don't rush yourself,' I said gently. 'And don't rush him. If this is meant to grow, it will. But even if it doesn't unfold exactly as you imagine, know this: You are not incomplete. A father can add to your life, yes. But he does not define your worth. You are already whole.'

I paused, then added with a faint smile, 'Perhaps that is what art is teaching you without you even realizing it—how to live with empty spaces, how to fill them with honesty, how to let them speak. Your longing for a father is like those lines on your page. It is not weakness, Ved. It is truth. And truth, when carried with patience, can one day become connection.'

He exhaled slowly, feeling a bit more comforted.

∼

All of us carry empty spaces in ourselves. For Ved, it was the absence of a father. For you, it may be something else—a parent's love you longed for but never fully received, a friendship that slipped away, a dream that never found its wings or a companionship that life did not allow you to hold close.

Our instinct is to try and fill these spaces quickly—with people, achievements, distractions. But the truth is not every space can or should be filled overnight. Some spaces must be honoured, acknowledged and lived with.

Empty spaces do not mean you are incomplete. They are the places where longing lives, where vulnerability breathes and where honesty is born.

The real wisdom is not in pretending those spaces don't exist, or in forcing someone or something to occupy them before its time. The wisdom is in learning to sit with them—to let them shape you, to let them soften you, to let them teach you patience.

Because when love does arrive, or when healing finally comes, it doesn't enter an empty void. It enters a heart that has already learned how to honour silence, how to wait and how to welcome without clinging.

So dear reader, if you feel the ache of an empty space in your own life, do not see it as a weakness. See it as an invitation to grow deeper, become gentler and create more room for grace.

One day, that space may be filled in ways you cannot imagine today. Or it may remain—but not as a wound, rather as soft ground where new life quietly takes root.

∽

Ved fidgeted with the corner of his sketchbook again, creasing the paper into a tired line. His foot tapped against the marble step, not in rhythm but with nerves. For a while, he said nothing.

When he finally spoke, his voice was quieter than I'd ever heard it. 'Gaurji …' He paused. 'There's something I've never told anyone. Not Mom, not even my closest friends.'

His eyes darted around, as if afraid that even the stone walls of the palace might overhear him.

'You know, it's funny,' he said with a nervous laugh, 'after hearing Mom cry with Dadi today … after watching them be so … raw … I thought, maybe I can also … say something I've kept buried inside for too long.' His laugh broke off. 'But I don't know. I'm scared.'

I didn't say a word.

Ved's grip tightened on his sketchbook. 'I'm scared because this isn't something I can take back once I say it. And it's not something I've even fully figured out for myself. But I trust you, Gaurji. You're … neutral. You're not inside the family drama, you don't have any expectations from me. And somehow … you make sense. You don't dismiss things.'

He took a shaky breath. 'So here it is … the first time I'm saying it out loud.' He stared down at his sneakers, his voice barely above a whisper, 'I think I'm gay.'

The words hovered in the air, trembling like a flame in a breeze.

He rushed on, almost tripping over his words. 'I haven't told Mom. I don't know how she'll react. I don't know how anyone will react. What if she thinks I'm broken? What if everyone looks at me differently? What if they're ashamed?' His fingers dug into the sketchbook's spine. 'Sometimes I even ask myself if it's real, or just a phase. And then I feel guilty for even being me.'

His chest rose and fell quickly. 'I've lived with this inside me for so long, I don't even know what freedom would feel like. I've thought about coming out, but then I freeze. I keep imagining the look on Mom's face. Or Nanu's. Or Nani's. Or Mama's. And I think ... maybe it's safer to just ... never say it.'

He lifted his eyes to mine.

When Ved shared his heart with me, I was reminded of something that has stayed with me for decades—a memory I wish I could rewrite.

Years ago, when I had just joined the ashram, I conducted a small weekly class for young people. One evening, after everyone else had left, a young man lingered behind. Nervous, hesitant, almost trembling, he finally opened up and told me something he had never told anyone else before. He said softly, 'I think I'm gay.'

It was his first act of real vulnerability. And what did I do? Instead of listening with compassion, I dismissed him. I told him to chant more, to read scriptures, to serve and that things would eventually be fine. That this phase—'being gay'—would somehow pass. My words weren't meant to hurt him, but they did.

That moment stayed with him. Many years later, long after he had built a successful career, I heard from a mutual friend that he still remembered the sting of my reaction. When his friend suggested reconnecting with me, he said, 'Not only do I not want to meet him, I don't even want to speak to him on the phone.'

That pierced me to the core. Because my failure had to do with not offering what every human being deserves when they share their heart—to be heard without judgement.

Of course, back then, I did the best I knew. Today, I know better—and so I try to do better. As Maya Angelou said: 'Do the best you can until you know better. Then when you know better, do better.'

And isn't that the truth of all our lives? We are all evolving. We are all works in progress.

And if we are all still learning, still becoming, then surely the least we can do is make it possible for one another to be honest without fear. To create safe spaces where people don't have to hide their truths, where they can show up as they are—vulnerable, imperfect, but real.

That is why judging others for the choices they make is never fair. After all, don't they say: 'Don't judge people for the choices they make when you don't know the options they had to choose from.'

Most of us carry burdens or truths that the world never sees. For some, it may be about who they love. For others, about the career they long for, the pain they've endured, their identity or the mistakes they regret making. And often, these truths remain hidden not because they are shameful, but because of fear—fear of how others will react, fear of being labelled, fear of being misunderstood.

The silence can feel safer, but it is heavy. It presses on the chest, it seeps into our smiles, it shapes our choices in ways we don't realize. To speak honestly, even once, is like exhaling after holding your breath underwater for too long.

Honesty takes courage. And courage doesn't mean being unafraid—it means being afraid and still speaking anyway.

This is why safe spaces matter. In our families, in our friendships, in our workplaces, people should not have to wear masks all the time. Creating such a space doesn't require grand speeches. It begins with simple acts—listening without rushing to fix, understanding before judging and telling someone quietly, 'You don't have to pretend with me.'

As I said earlier, and I repeat, if for some reason we cannot open our truths to others, we can still be honest with ourselves. Or if faith gives us strength, we can pour our truths out in prayer to God. Even that act of admitting it to ourselves or offering it to the Divine lightens the weight, loosens the silence and begins the healing.

So ask yourself: Am I creating a space where honesty can live? And equally: Am I giving myself permission to be honest, at least with myself?

Because one day, when the truths we carry inside us are finally spoken out aloud, we will discover something powerful—the world does not break when we become real. Instead, our hearts grow lighter and our relationships deepen.

∼

I let his words hang in the air for a moment, not rushing to fill the silence. Then I said softly, 'Ved ... do you realize how much courage it takes to do what you just did? To give voice to something you've carried inside for so long? That in itself is an act of strength.'

He blinked, unsure, as though waiting for judgement.

'I'm not here to label you or define you,' I continued. 'But I want you to know this: nothing about what you've said makes you broken. Instead, it makes you human. Just like everyone else—with their longings, truths and fears. And being honest about your truth is not shameful. It is sacred.'

Ved's eyes welled up, but he kept looking steadily at me.

'I can understand why you're scared,' I said. 'You wonder how your mom will take it, how your family or friends will respond. Those are real fears. And it's wise of you to think carefully about when and how to share something so precious. But remember—this truth is not a burden. It is not something to apologize for. It is a part of who you are.'

He looked down at the sketchbook still clenched in his hands.

'You know what I see in your art, Ved?' I asked gently. 'A boy under a dark sky with an umbrella too small, a bird straining against its cage ... those are not just drawings. They are the ways in which your heart is expressing itself when your lips cannot. You've already been honest. And today, you took the next step.'

I leaned in slightly. 'Coming out—that's not a performance for others. It's not about blurting it out because you feel pressured. It's about choosing a moment, in a way and at a place where your heart feels safe. It's about when you are ready. And readiness doesn't mean you're fearless—it means you're tired of hiding from yourself.'

Ved's breath shuddered, and something inside him seemed to shift.

'So here's what I'll say,' I continued, my voice calm. 'Don't measure yourself by how others might respond. Their reactions belong to them, not to you. Your truth belongs to you. Whether you choose to share it tomorrow, next year or only with those you truly trust, that's your decision. What matters is that you don't lose yourself in the fear of how the world will see you.'

I paused, then smiled gently. 'And Ved … if your mom has taught you anything, it's that love can be fierce, even when it struggles at first. She may need time, she may stumble with her own expectations, but a mother's heart doesn't stop loving because her child is honest. Give her, and yourself, that grace.'

Something in him quietly relaxed, and he let out a breath he hadn't realized he had been holding.

∼

The last of the afternoon light drenched the palace walls. Ved tucked his sketchbook back into his tote, brushing the dust off his kurta as he stood up. For a moment, we lingered on the steps—it was very still, as if the stone itself had absorbed the gravity of what had been shared. He breathed out, a hint of ease returning, and managed a small smile.

'Come on, Gaurji,' he said, half-grinning, 'if we sit here any longer, Dadi will personally drag us to the haldi and make us her canvas.'

We laughed and walked back together towards the courtyard that looked like it had been dipped in turmeric. Yellow drapes cascaded from the arches, marigold garlands crisscrossed overhead and brass plates shone with golden paste. Buckets of water stood ready in one corner—officially for 'emergencies', though everyone knew they were really ammunition.

Rukmini Dadi, dressed in a bright mustard sari that perfectly matched the occasion, surveyed the scene like a general preparing for battle. 'Arré, listen everyone!' she yelled at the decorators still fussing with the cushions. 'No need for symmetry. By the time these monkeys are done, it will look like Holi anyway!'

Everyone laughed, though the decorators looked faintly offended.

Rakesh entered with Lakshmi at his side, both trying to look dignified in their neatly pressed kurtas—a dignity that lasted precisely two minutes, until a cousin came racing past with a handful of turmeric and nearly smeared it across Rakesh's face. He ducked just in time, but Lakshmi wasn't so lucky. A bright yellow streak landed squarely on her cheek.

'Arré!' she yelped, glaring at Rakesh. 'This is your family's mischief!'

Rakesh raised his hands in protest, grinning. 'Don't blame me—blame the haldi traditions!'

Gaurav arrived soon after, rolling up his sleeves, already prepared. 'If I'm going to be dragged into this, I'd rather look ready for a wrestling match,' he joked. Priya, standing beside him in a pale yellow salwar suit, tried to maintain her composure, until Rukmini Dadi winked and announced loudly, 'Priya beta, you'd better stand close to him. People are aiming at you, but they might miss on purpose and hit him!'

The courtyard erupted in laughter. Priya turned crimson, Gaurav chuckled and Ved muttered dramatically, 'Dadi needs a filter,' which only made everyone laugh harder.

Meanwhile, Rohan and Sanjana were seated like royalty on low wooden stools, surrounded by friends and cousins who were already singing playful songs. Sanjana tried to maintain her poise, but her dupatta had been pulled off her shoulder within seconds, and Rohan's kurta had its first yellow handprint before he could even sit properly.

'See?' Rohan said, holding up his hands in mock surrender. 'This is not a haldi. This is organized bullying!'

One of his friends shouted back, 'Of course! That's the whole point!'

Within moments, the ceremony had dissolved into a free-for-all. Friends and cousins leapt forward with bowls, aunts exchanged sly glances before attacking each other and little kids ran in circles trying to smear turmeric on anyone slow enough to be caught.

Priya, trying to escape unnoticed, was ambushed by Gaurav, who gently dabbed a bit of turmeric on her forehead. She looked at him in surprise and, for a brief moment amidst the laughter and chaos, their gaze met—soft, steady.

By the end, the courtyard looked exactly as Dadi had predicted: a battlefield of yellow streaks, laughter echoing off the walls and everyone glowing like sunflowers in bloom. The sacred had mingled with the silly, the ritual with the riot—and in that mess of turmeric, joy had left its indelible mark.

Had it, though? Or was it only on the surface—a golden glow carefully guarding what stirred beneath?

Would the haldi—meant to cleanse, to bless, to prepare—also heal what words had not yet managed to? Would it draw Rohan and Sanjana closer, or simply cover the cracks with colour too bright to last?

As the evening drew to a close and the joyful scenes from the haldi flitted through my head, I was reminded that life, like relationships, is held together not by perfection but by honesty.

When Ved spoke to me that afternoon, his voice low and uncertain, something within me stirred. There was a trembling honesty in his words—the kind that comes only when a heart decides to stop hiding. His confession wasn't about right or wrong, it was about being seen.

I found myself listening—not as a teacher, not as a monk, but as a fellow human being. Years ago, I might have filled that silence with advice or verses. But this time, I simply sat with him, allowing his truth to breathe. In that quiet, I understood something—that love isn't about correcting someone's path, it's about walking beside them while they find their own.

In Ved's confession, I felt an ache—a mix of tenderness and humility. He had trusted me with his truth, and in that trust, I felt a quiet redemption—as if life had circled back to offer me another chance to help the right way.

....

THINGS TO THINK ABOUT ...

HALDI AS A METAPHOR: What haldi does for the skin, forgiveness does for the heart—it heals, it softens, it restores. And kindness, like a gentle balm, keeps love from hardening into hurt.

SAFE SPACES FOR TRUTH: Vulnerability blooms when one is able to listen without rushing, be present without judgement and honour the timing chosen by the heart. The truth should be shared when one feels safe and ready.

DIFFICULT CHOICES: Sometimes it isn't about right or wrong. It's about choosing what hurts a little less.

THE CROSSROADS OF RIGHT AND WRONG: Sometimes life asks us to choose between two 'rights'. The better question is: Which choice gives me inner peace? Own the choice with honesty, and dignity will follow.

LIVING WITH EMPTY SPACES: Not every longing needs to be instantly gratified. Some spaces must be honoured—not hidden—until love or healing arrives. Authenticity is wholeness, not flawlessness.

HONESTY AS HEALING: Confessing (about a buried truth) is not a weakness—it's cleansing. When truths are brought into light with care, shame is loosened, dignity returns and we can step forward with clarity.

•••••••••••••••

The exercises related to the concepts mentioned in this chapter can be found on p. 278.

9

Unfinished Stories
Finding Clarity without Closure

~

Not every chapter in life closes neatly, some stay
open as lessons.
The goal is not perfect closure but clear vision—
for when the mind is calm and the heart is honest,
even unfinished moments can show us the way
forward.

We speak so much about 'closure', as if everything painful can be neatly sealed and filed away like a lawsuit settled or a business deal signed. But real life rarely offers such tidy endings. Instead, it leaves us with reminders. A day, a place, a person or even a smell can suddenly trigger what we thought we had locked away. And what we believed was over comes alive again—sometimes leaving us disturbed, sometimes confused and sometimes helpless.

Every time I land at Heathrow in London, I am reminded of this truth. Every city has a familiar smell that can transport us back in time—to memories good or bad, or a mix of both; some faint, some sharp, depending on our experiences there. Heathrow has its own peculiar atmosphere—there's the faint chill that greets you as you step off the aircraft, the smell of roasted coffee wafting out from the kiosks, the sterile smell of the long polished corridors, the muffled announcements echoing across terminals and, of course, the serpentine queues at immigration. For most travellers, Heathrow is just an airport. For me, it has always been a portal—a doorway to years of service, friendship and learning at Bhaktivedanta Manor.

The Manor itself is worlds away from Heathrow. Once owned by George Harrison of the Beatles and later gifted to the International Society for Krishna Consciousness, this sprawling estate in Hertfordshire is where English-countryside charm and timeless Indian devotion come together. There are rolling green fields, ponds with gliding swans, a winding driveway leading up to the red-brick manor house and, beyond it, the temple hall that has witnessed countless prayers, kirtans, lectures and the tears of seekers searching for the truth. The air there is its own perfume—incense mingling with fresh grass. Bells echo across the meadows, and the quiet hum of chanting fills the air.

For several weeks every year, from 2006–19, I stayed there. My dear friends Srutidharma Das and Pranabandhu Das would pick me up from Heathrow, their smiles warm enough to dissolve the weariness of the long flight. I can still recall our conversations in the car—laughter, reflections and plans for the days ahead. The devotees in the ashram welcomed me with a simplicity reserved for family, and the congregation families extended so much love that one could only feel deeply grateful. Those visits were not just opportunities to share my thoughts in lectures and seminars at homes, universities, community halls and the temple itself. They were moments of immense enrichment—when I deepened my own understanding of life and spirituality while helping others explore theirs.

Those years remain among the most precious times of my life—characterized by deep bonds, shared service, kindness freely given and love freely received. Even today, when I pass through Heathrow, nostalgia rises in me—not as a vague sentiment but as a wave of gratitude, joy and quiet satisfaction that such love and learning were once part of my journey.

But the colours of reminiscences are not always golden. Visiting the Manor also stirs up a memory that stings. I recall a senior lady, much older to me, who once severely chastised me—humiliating me, though thankfully in private—for something I had said during a morning talk. She asked me to publicly apologize in the evening session before 150–200 people. I did not know her personally; this was my very first interaction with her. Perhaps she was right from her perspective, perhaps I was right from mine—but right and wrong are not the point here. What stayed with me was not the content of the correction, but the way it was delivered. Sharp. Harsh. Wounding.

Now, can I erase that memory? No. Can I say it's gone? No. Will it be triggered if I see her? Yes. That is life.

And yet, I choose not to hold the memory with arrogance or resentment. Because I chose humility over defensiveness. I apologized, not because I felt defeated, but because I valued peace over proving a point. I used the moment as an opportunity to work on myself—to become more sensitive with my words, more careful with my tone. Every time that memory resurfaces, it brings with it the sting, yes, but also the learning.

Of course, there will be other times in life when humility must take a different form—not silent acceptance, but the courage to speak, to stand one's ground, even to prove a point. To defend oneself or one's values is not arrogance when it comes from a place of clarity, not ego. Wisdom lies in discerning when peace can be preserved by stepping back—or stepping forward.

And so, as the courtyard outside was being prepared for the wedding with flowers and sacred fire, I was reminded that every ritual—like every memory—carries its traces into what comes next. The question is not whether the past will reappear, but whether love will be strong enough, and truthful enough, to meet it when it does.

∽

The palace hummed like a beehive, every corner buzzing with urgency or laughter. Children leaned over balconies, their fists tight around paper cones filled with flower petals, plotting their ambush of the groom's procession. Near the entrance, a cluster of cousins argued over who had the best dance moves.

'Bro, I've been practising for weeks,' one boasted.

Another snorted, 'Practising? It's a baraat, not a reality show!'

Inside, the band tested their dhols and trumpets with noisy bursts that startled the pigeons off the palace roof. An uncle muttered, 'Arré bhai, is this a wedding or a political rally?' But even he couldn't hide his grin.

Then, with a clash of cymbals and the first full-bodied crack of the dhols, the gates opened. Horns blared, music erupted and, suddenly, the morning's quiet anticipation exploded into loud celebration.

The cousins were the first to leap forward, arms flying, legs stomping, each convinced that they were the star of the show. Uncles clapped gamely, some valiantly attempting a shoulder shrug or sideways shuffle, while others swayed in place, careful not to test their knees too much. The aunts clustered together, singing traditional wedding songs, laughing and offering live commentary on everyone's moves.

At the centre of it all stood the white mare, draped in velvet edged with golden tassels. Rohan, dressed in his ivory sherwani and saffron turban, stepped forward, flanked by his cousins; together, they looked like a cricket team entering the field. The mare snorted, as though she too understood the importance of her role.

'Hold him tight!' a friend called out dramatically. 'If he slips, we'll have to find a new groom before lunch!'

There were roars of laughter as Rohan mounted the mare—awkward for a second, then steadying himself into the posture he'd probably imagined himself in a hundred times before but never rehearsed.

The baraat surged forward in a wave of noise and colour.

Above the swirl of the drums and the dancing, Rukmini Dadi had shifted to the balcony, leaning over the railing, her dupatta flapping like a flag in the breeze. She cupped her hands to her mouth and boomed, '*Arré, dulhe raja, thoda muskurao! Bandwalon ko daraoge kya* [Hey, groom, smile a little! Else you will scare the musicians in the procession]!'

Her words fell on the baraat like petals tossed from above. Even the band broke rhythm for a moment, the trumpeters grinning at the funny interruption.

Rohan, perched tall on his white mare, broke into a broad smile—the kind that drew fresh cheers from everyone around and satisfied Dadi's playful command. She nodded triumphantly from above, as though she had personally restored the sparkle of the celebration.

Priya watched quietly from one side of the courtyard, her gaze more on the crowd than the groom. Gaurav slipped beside her and murmured, 'Looks like the real competition is between the guests and the band—who can be louder?' She laughed softly, her eyes warming for a moment.

Lakshmi and Rakesh stood near the entrance, poised, the official hosts. Lakshmi adjusted the edge of her sari, whispering a prayer, while Rakesh clapped with a group of uncles, half-hiding his nervousness with humour. 'I think the horse looks calmer than the groom,' he quipped, earning a round of hearty laughter.

The baraat inched forward in joyous chaos—drums thundering, petals raining from the balconies, friends dancing like there was no tomorrow. Uncoordinated, noisy, overflowing, but that was the point. A baraat was never meant to march straight—it was meant to declare joy, to embrace the mess, to celebrate life in all its unruly abundance.

Just then the dhols thundered louder, the mare stamped her hooves and the baraat moved closer towards the palace gates.

Women in bright saris lined the entrance, their decked thalis ready, lamps flickering bravely in the cool desert breeze. The fragrance of incense mingled with marigolds as they began the aarti, circling the groom with blessings and songs. The children, unable to contain their excitement, darted forward too soon, tossing petals into the air with triumphant squeals. A shower of red and yellow rained down on Rohan and his mare, who flicked her ears in dignified disapproval.

Just as the priest intoned some Sanskrit mantras, a cheeky boy leapt up, supported by a few other cousins, and tugged at Rohan's nose—the traditional reminder that however regal the groom looked atop the horse, he must enter the bride's home with humility.

'Ow!' Rohan exclaimed in mock pain, rubbing his nose dramatically. The crowd roared. 'Good omen!' someone shouted. 'The *dulha's naak* has already been bent.'

The real battle, however, was happening a few steps behind the scene. A huddle of younger cousins, with conspiratorial whispers and exaggerated hand signals, were plotting their mission: to hide the groom's shoes.

'Okay, you distract the uncles. I'll slip in under the horse,' one whispered.

'Under the horse?!' the other hissed back. 'You want to start the ceremony with a hospital visit?'

Ved, of course, was providing live commentary, phone in hand. 'Operation Joota Chhupai is underway,' he whispered like a war correspondent reporting from the front line. 'Decoy team advancing … Diversion team holding position near the jalebi counter … Success probability: 50 per cent, unless Dadi intervenes.'

The gates of the palace—now more theatre than threshold—opened wide, ready to swallow the noise, the rituals, the joy and a great deal more. Guests streamed in, decked out beautifully, laughter and greetings tumbling together in the air.

It felt like a curtain was being lifted. The baraat spilled through, dhols pounding, cousins twirling, banter flying across the courtyard towards the centre where the mandap stood draped in jasmine and roses. Above, a canopy of silk shimmered in shades of ivory and crimson, catching the light like a blessing woven into the fabric. At its heart sat the havan kund, a square of firewood carefully arranged, waiting to be lit—the sacred flame that would serve as both witness and purifier.

Priests bustled about, their voices weaving Sanskrit verses into the air as they arranged trays of rice, ghee, camphor and sandalwood. Each object was there for a reason: rice for prosperity, ghee for sustenance, camphor for cleansing, fire for truth. None of it was meant as mere ritual—each was a reminder that love too requires nourishment, sacrifice and clarity.

The guests found their places in neat rows, their vibrant saris and kurtas forming a sea of colour. Children wriggled impatiently in their seats, some already trying to sneak laddus from the trays meant for offerings. The uncles whispered to one another about the decor, the aunts hummed familiar shaadi songs under their breath and, in quiet corners, the elders closed their eyes, lost in prayer.

The groom entered the mandap first, his stride steady, his smile greeted with cheers. Friends teased him, cousins straightened his safa with exaggerated seriousness and someone whispered a joke that made him laugh out loud.

And then came the bride.

Sanjana appeared at the far end of the courtyard, draped in crimson and gold, her veil catching the morning light like a flame being carried forward. Each step she took was measured, graceful yet heavy with the weight of all that this moment meant. Around her, friends fussed with her dupatta and children scattered petals before her feet.

Gaurav walked beside her, holding her hand firmly, steadying her through the tremor of nerves that even the most radiant bride cannot fully hide.

He thought of his parents—gone too soon—and how he had once been a twenty-one-year-old boy suddenly thrust into the roles of father, mother, provider and protector. He thought of the nights he had stayed awake by Sanjana's side when she was ill, of the jobs he had taken while still a student just to fund her dreams, of the laughter he had forced out of himself when all he wanted was to break down. Every sacrifice, every compromise, every silent prayer had been for this: Sanjana's happiness, her future, her chance to stand here today—not as an orphaned girl but as a cherished bride.

The courtyard seemed to grow still as they approached the mandap. The dhol beats softened, the chatter dimmed and, for a moment, it felt as though the entire gathering had stepped aside to make space for the bond between a brother and sister. Gaurav lifted Sanjana's veil slightly, tucking a stray lock of hair behind her ear, his smile trembling but tender.

As they reached the mandap, he paused. For a brief second, he closed his eyes, almost as though he were speaking silently to his parents—I did it. She's safe, she's happy, she's ready for her new home. Then, with both pride and reluctance, he placed Sanjana's hand into the priest's waiting one, and guided her gently towards the seat beside her groom.

Sanjana glanced at him, her eyes glistening with tears, and whispered so softly that only he could hear: 'Thank you ... for being everything to me.' Gaurav squeezed her hand one last time, with the memories of all their years together filling his mind, before stepping back.

And in that moment, the courtyard witnessed something bigger than any ritual—the quiet, unspoken power of love that does not demand, does not boast, but simply gives.

As Gaurav stepped back, eyes still moist, Rukmini Dadi's voice boomed from the front row: '*Bas, bas! Gaurav beta, ab rona dhona band karo. Yeh toh dulhan hai, sasural jaa rahi hai—tumhari vidaai thodi na ho rahi hai* [Enough, Gaurav! Stop crying now. She's the bride going to her in-laws' home—it's not *your* farewell]!'

The crowd erupted in laughter, even as Gaurav wiped his eyes sheepishly, caught between embarrassment and affection.

As I watched the courtyard sway between tears and laughter, I was reminded of that immortal song from the film *Anand* (1971):

Zindagi kaisi hai paheli haaye,
Kabhi toh hasaye, kabhi yeh rulaaye ...

What a riddle life truly is. Sometimes it lifts us into peals of laughter, and sometimes it leaves us trembling with tears.

And yet, it is in this rhythm—between joy and sorrow, between smiles and sobs—that life finds its fullness.

Laughter is a gift. It lightens the air, breaks walls and makes us forget, even if for a moment, the heaviness we carry. It elevates us, like helium lifting a balloon skyward. Who doesn't love the sound of shared laughter echoing in a hall, or the way a joke melts away the ice?

But as beautiful as laughter is, it is often the tears that touch us more deeply. Not just the tears shed over problems or losses—though, those too are necessary—but the tears that come when something pierces the heart. When love overwhelms us, when gratitude spills over, when sacrifice is recognized, when someone's truth resonates with our own. Those tears cleanse. They stir the soul. They remind us that beneath our busyness, we are human, tender, alive.

And isn't that balance necessary? Too much sweetness, and life would become cloying, even dangerous—just as too much sugar causes disease. Too much sorrow, and we would break under the weight. But the mix—a spoonful of sweetness and a dash of bitterness—makes the meal nourishing. The laughter is our rasgulla, and the tears are our karela—together, they complete the thali.

Life, like the song says, is a riddle not meant to be solved, but savoured. The joy of seeing Gaurav's tears of fulfilment and Dadi's thunderous humour in the same breath—that was not contradiction, it was harmony. Because to be fully human is to give both their place.

So let us not resist either. Laugh when life gives us a reason to laugh. Cry when the heart is touched. And know that in both—the sweet and the bitter, the rasgulla and the karela—lies the strange, magnificent wholeness of life.

∼

Just as the courtyard settled down and the priests began their chants, one of them paused, peered at his almanac and cleared his throat.

'*Arré, dulha-dulhan ki baarat toh time se pehle aa gayi* [Oh, the bride and groom's baraat has arrived earlier than expected],' he announced, half-amused, half-surprised. 'For once in history, everything is ahead of schedule. But the *muhurat* for the *pheras* … *woh toh abhi kuch der baad hai* [that is still a little while away].'

The crowd laughed. An uncle clapped his hands and said, 'Wah, miracles do happen! This family has broken the record for punctuality.'

The priest, smiling at the commotion, added diplomatically, 'Since there is some time, the bride and groom may take a short break. They can freshen up, have some water and return closer to the time of the muhurat.'

The families nodded in agreement, and the buzz of conversation picked up again. Guests stretched their legs, the aunts swapped gossip, the uncles discussed the stock market and the children darted off in search of more laddus. To everyone else, it was a natural pause, nothing unusual at all.

It was then that Rohan turned towards me, his voice steady but his eyes saying more than words could.

'Swamiji ... before the rituals begin, could Sanjana and I spend a few minutes with you? Just for your blessings.'

Smiles followed them as the young couple slipped away with me—but beneath that facade, only I knew that what they were dealing with wasn't just about garlands and rituals—they had questions that needed answering before the vows could be spoken.

We slipped through a side corridor lined with bougainvillea, the sound of dhols and chatter dimming with every step. For a moment, it felt as if the palace itself was holding its breath, waiting to overhear what was about to be discussed.

Rohan released Sanjana's hand, only to fold his palms before me. His voice was steady, respectful, but his eyes betrayed a restlessness beneath the calm. His chest rose and fell more quickly than his words did, and his jaw tightened as though he was holding back more than he wished to say.

'Swamiji,' he began, his voice catching slightly, 'everyone thinks we're here for your blessings. And we are. But ... there's something more we need to share.'

Sanjana lowered her gaze, her veil trembling as she exhaled. Her fingers toyed nervously with her bangles. She glanced at Rohan, then at me, her lips parting, as if unsure whether her voice would carry. Finally, she spoke, each word careful, deliberate, fragile.

'We've spoken, Swamiji. Last night ... honestly. About everything. About Karan. About trust. About fear.'

Rohan's hands clenched for a moment at his side, then loosened as though he was forcing himself to remain composed. He looked somewhere beyond my shoulder.

'I thought I was ready,' he admitted, his voice lower now. 'I wanted to be. But when I saw how easily a shadow could enter, how quickly trust could tremble, I realized that marriage isn't something we can step into just because the mandap is decorated and the priest says it is time.'

He paused, struggling to meet my eyes. The silence between us deepened. The fragrance of jasmine floated in on the breeze, contrasting sharply with the heaviness of his words.

'We didn't come to you earlier,' he continued, his voice firmer now, 'because, truthfully, we weren't sure until last night. We kept hoping that the tide of celebration—the haldi, the mehendi, the music—would steady us. That by the time the day arrived, we would feel ready. But when we spoke alone, we realized the truth—our love is strong, but our foundation still needs time to strengthen.'

Sanjana's eyes glistened. She blinked back the tears that clung stubbornly to her lashes. Her words, when they came, were soft, yet resolute.

'We do love each other,' she whispered. 'That much is clear. But we also know that love alone isn't enough if it can be shaken so quickly. We don't want to make promises about what we can't protect. We don't want to take our vows today, only to discover tomorrow that we weren't ready to honour them.'

Her words hung between us, as fragile and heavy as glass.

The sounds of drums, laughter and the occasional shout of children could be heard faintly in the distance, but here, in this corridor, they felt worlds away. Time seemed to be suspended.

Rohan finally turned his eyes to mine. Something in his posture gave way, the tension in his body softening.

'So Swamiji …' he said, his voice quiet but steady, 'we've decided we want time. Not to run away. Not to break up. But to build up. To work on ourselves and each other more, to understand more deeply, to strengthen what we have before binding it together with sacred vows.'

Sanjana, still blinking back the torrent of unshed tears threatening to flow out, nodded faintly.

'We're committed to each other,' she said softly. 'We just don't want to begin with pretence. We want to begin with the truth.'

I let their words hang in the air for a while.

Finally, I spoke. My voice was gentle, but each word carried the gravity of what they had just entrusted me with.

'What you have done now, Rohan and Sanjana, is braver than exchanging vows in front of hundreds of people. It is easy to walk the seven steps when the music is playing, when everyone is clapping, when the fire burns bright. It is easy to smile for the cameras, to follow the priest's instructions, to let rituals carry you forward even if your hearts hesitate. But to pause? To stop amidst the tide of expectations and admit, We are not ready—that takes a different kind of strength. That takes courage, the kind most people never discover in themselves.'

Rohan's shoulders eased a little, but his eyes were still heavy with unspoken thoughts. His voice broke softly, 'But Swamiji ... won't people say we failed?'

I shook my head slowly, a small smile on my lips. 'No, Rohan. There is no failure in choosing honesty. Failure is in pretending, in performing vows your heart cannot yet stand by. A ritual isn't sacred just because it's performed—it becomes sacred when the hearts behind it are prepared. Vows are not strings that tie two people together, they are living promises that must be carried out with patience, tenderness and truth. If you had taken them today without being fully ready, that would have been a betrayal. Not towards society or family, but towards yourselves.'

Sanjana dabbed her eyes with the edge of her dupatta. Her voice trembled. 'We just don't want to hurt our families. They've dreamt of this day for so long.'

I leaned forward, my gaze tender but firm. 'And that is why you must tell them of your decision respectfully. You must come from a place of reverence, not rebellion. Families invest not only in rituals but in dreams—and yes, they will feel that their dreams have been shaken to the core. Yes, they will be shocked. Some may even be angry. But in time, they will see what I see—that you are not walking away from each other, you are walking, more carefully, *towards* each other. That this is not a rejection of love, but its truest expression—to wait until you are strong enough to truly honour the vows you hope to make one day.'

Just for a moment, their breathing steadied—the heaviness hadn't gone away, but it no longer pressed down so hard. The weight was still there, but it was no longer crushing them. The clouds still hung overhead, but the thunder had eased.

'Come,' I said softly, 'let us bring in those who must know—not the whole courtyard just yet, only those closest to you. Gaurav, Lakshmi, Rakesh, Priya and, of course, Dadi. Their shoulders are strong enough to bear this truth with you. And their love for you is deeper than their expectations.'

Both of them nodded slowly. Rohan pressed his palms together, his voice hushed but steady. 'Thank you, Swamiji. We wanted blessings … this feels like one too.'

Worse than the lies we tell others are the lies we tell ourselves. Because when we lie to others, somewhere deep inside we still know the truth. But when we lie to ourselves, we bury the truth so far down that even we stop recognizing it.

And isn't that what we often do in relationships, in careers, in our daily lives? We stay where we don't belong, or we rush into what we are not yet ready for—just because admitting the truth to ourselves feels like too much to bear. Many are scared of ghosts, even though we are not sure if they exist at all. But we have no fear of the demons within, the demons of denial, pretence, avoidance. The only way forward is to face those inner demons with honesty.

When we are honest with ourselves, uncomfortable as it may be, we begin to see. The fog clears. But when we deceive ourselves—telling ourselves that we are ready when we are not, that we are happy when we are broken and that we can endure what we clearly cannot—we condemn ourselves to repeat cycles that wound us further.

Being honest with ourselves is the starting point of wisdom. Without it, every decision becomes an escape, not a choice.

That's why stillness matters. Silence matters. Honest conversations matter. Too often, we make decisions simply to quiet the noise within, to find temporary relief from restlessness. But decisions made in agitation rarely serve us well. Imagine a lake in turbulent weather—its waters muddy, wild ripples, surface broken. Look into it and what will you see? Nothing clear, only distorted reflections. In the same way, when our minds are unsettled, whichever direction we choose to go in—to stay, to leave, to say yes, to say no—is more likely to be a blunder. But when the wind ceases and the ripples fade, the lake becomes a mirror. That is when clarity appears.

And that is what Rohan and Sanjana chose. There was no perfect closure to what they were going through. The ghosts of the past had resurfaced, shadows lingered, questions remained. But instead of rushing forward into vows under pressure, they paused. They allowed their inner lake to settle. And coming from that place of clarity, they chose honesty. They did not escape from the situation but chose to act with wisdom.

Of course, in such moments, guidance helps. Elders, mentors, friends can help illuminate paths we may not be able to see. They can steady us when we tremble, warn us of our mistakes. But here is the truth: Guidance is meant to facilitate clarity, not replace it. Others can advise, but they do not have to live our lives. We have to. So while advice can guide us, only our inner voice must decide—because only we must bear the consequences.

So no, Rohan and Sanjana did not get closure in the way people usually seek it—neat endings, tidy answers. What they got was clarity. And that clarity, born of stillness and honesty, is often more powerful than closure. It doesn't get rid of the ghosts, but it teaches us how to live bravely with them.

And when it comes to others—the world, society, even family—any applause or criticism is always temporary. What the world thinks of our decisions matters far less than what we think of our own lives. At the end of the day, we must live with ourselves.

Yet when an explanation is needed—especially for the sake of those who love us and have invested in us—it must be given not to justify but to honour their concern. With gentleness, not defensiveness. That is when the truth transforms from a sword into a bridge.

•••••••••••••••

THINGS TO THINK ABOUT ...

CLOSURE IN LIFE IS RARELY NEAT OR FINAL: Memories don't fade, they wait. And one day, they return—reminding us of unfinished stories. The test of wisdom is not in forgetting those stories, but in integrating them into our lives: choosing humility over resentment, knowing when to step back or stand firm, and in relationships, facing lingering shadows together with honesty and love. True closure is not a deletion of the memory but allowing transformation to happen because of it—letting old stains become a part of the fabric that strengthens the bond.

LIFE'S BEAUTY LIES IN ITS CONTRASTS—IN THE LAUGHTER THAT LIFTS US AND THE TEARS THAT CLEANSE US: Joy makes us light, but it is pain that makes us deep. Just as a meal needs both sweetness and bitterness to be whole, our hearts need both laughter and tears to stay alive. To live fully is not to choose one over the other, but to embrace both—the rasgulla and the karela—as the essential flavours of a complete life.

HONESTY WITH OURSELVES: Clarity comes the moment we stop lying to ourselves. When we stop pretending—to be fine, to be ready, to be strong—the fog starts to lift. But when we live behind illusions, we keep spinning inside the same old storms. To be truthful with oneself is the first act of wisdom. Everything else grows from there.

WISE DECISIONS ARE NOT MADE IN MOMENTS OF TURBULENCE BUT IN MOMENTS OF CLARITY: Like a lake that reflects only when its waters are still, our minds too must settle before we decide what to do in difficult moments. Guidance can illuminate the way, but the final decision must come from within, because we alone have to face its consequences. Decisions rooted in honesty and readiness may not please everyone, but they preserve one's dignity and build bridges of trust.

•••••••••••••••

The exercises related to the concepts mentioned in this chapter can be found on p. 282.

10

A WELL-BAKED CAKE

Aligning Thought and Action

~

Endless thinking without action leads to stagnation. Reckless action without reflection leads to destruction. Wisdom is the art of aligning the two.

The corridor stirred with the sound of footsteps. One by one they came—Gaurav first, his brow furrowed in curiosity; Lakshmi followed close behind, her sari pleats rustling as though they could sense her nervousness. Rakesh walked with the stiff dignity of a man accustomed to answers, not mysteries. Priya slipped in quietly, her eyes scanning the room with a habitual alertness. And last came Dadi, leaning on her stick, her presence filling the space more than the beat of any dhol outside.

Their faces still shone with the glow of festivity, unaware that their day was about to turn upside down. To the world outside, it must have looked like the family was gathering for a few private moments before the rituals. But inside, the air had thickened.

Gaurav was the first to notice the unease. His eyes darted between Rohan and Sanjana, before he turned to me. 'Swamiji … *sab theek hai na?*'

I raised a hand gently, signalling for calm. 'Yes, Gaurav. Everything is fine. But the bride and groom wish to speak truthfully before we step further. Don't worry, they are not running away from each other. In fact, they are choosing each other—but with honesty, not haste.'

Lakshmi stiffened. Her hand went instinctively to her chest. '*Kya matlab*, Swamiji?' Her voice was a whisper; her eyes pleaded for clarity.

Sanjana lowered her eyes. Rohan's grip on her hand was firm, though a faint tremor ran through his fingers. He took a long breath, then spoke.

'Ma, Papa … Sanjana and I love each other. That has never been in doubt. But last night, for the first time, we spoke with each other with complete honesty—about our fears, our doubts, the trust we still need to build. And we realized something neither of us can ignore.

'Marriage is not just about rituals and music. It is about the vows that must last a lifetime. And if we take these vows today, in this moment, with these questions still between us, we will be breaking them before they are even spoken. That would be a betrayal—not only of each other, but of you, of this sacred fire, of God.'

Sanjana's voice, soft but steady, followed, 'We don't want to stand before the sacred flame with hesitation in our hearts. We want to come to it in truth, not with pretence. This is not rejection … this is respect. Respect for marriage, respect for you and respect for the vows themselves.'

Her words landed like stones in still water, casting ripples of silence that spread across the room.

Lakshmi was the first to break. 'What are you saying?' Her voice rose, then cracked. 'The mandap is ready, our relatives are waiting … After all the preparations, all the hopes, *now* you say you're not ready?' Tears streamed down her face as she shook her head in disbelief.

Rakesh's jaw tightened. He stood straighter, his words clipped, hiding restrained anger. 'Do you even realize what you're saying? The courtyard is full of guests, the priests are ready and everyone's eyes are on us. This family's honour is at stake. You think when people get married they are absolutely certain of each other? Every couple enters into the bond with questions in their mind. No one is ever fully ready. You step in, and you grow into it. That is how life works.'

Gaurav's voice, usually calm, cut through next, sharper than he perhaps intended, 'Rohan. Sanjana. This sounds vague. Fears? Trust? Everyone has fears, everyone works on trust. Tell us plainly—what is the real reason? Because to stop a wedding at the mandap, there has to be more.' He looked at his sister and Rohan.

Priya sat wordless, her hands folded tightly in her lap. Her eyes reflected compassion but also confusion. She glanced once at Sanjana, then at me, as if to ask silently: Is this really happening?

And then Dadi's walking stick struck the floor, sharp against the stone. Her eyes blazed. '*Pagal ho gaye ho tum dono* [Have you both gone mad]! At the very mandap you decide to do this?' She leaned forward, her voice trembling with fury. 'Do you know what uproar this will cause? Guests will talk, tongues will wag; this family's name will be dragged through the mud for years. You think honesty is easy? Honesty comes at a price!'

The room fell into a stunned hush. Outside, the dhols still pounded, the laughter still echoed—but here, time stood still.

Sanjana's tears finally spilled over. She gripped Rohan's hand tighter, her lips trembling. In a whisper, almost to herself, she said, 'Better an uproar today … than regret tomorrow.'

I raised my hand, letting the silence settle before I spoke.

'Rakeshji, you are right—every couple enters marriage with questions. Doubts are natural. But there is a difference between questions that can be carried together and cracks that must be healed first. Marriage is not a plaster that hides a wound, it is a bond that magnifies it. If they walk into the mandap with hesitation, the vows will not clarify their feelings. Instead, the fire will only deepen the cracks. They are not saying they don't want to marry. They are saying they want to enter into marriage when their hearts are whole enough to keep the promises.'

I turned to Gaurav, whose eyes still searched for a deeper reason. His love for his sister was fierce, but his suspicion sharper still.

'Gaurav, I understand your question: What is the real reason? You are protective—as Sanjana's brother, as her family you want to know what reasons lie behind these words. Let me tell you this—not every truth is meant to be shouted across a crowded courtyard. Some truths must be tended to like a flame until they are steady enough to be seen in the open. Rohan and Sanjana have spoken their truth to me, and I assure you, it is not about betrayal, nor about walking away. It is about honouring the vows rather than performing them superficially. Sometimes honesty is not the whole explanation, sometimes it is simply the courage to say, We are not ready yet.'

I looked at them all, letting my words rest in the silence.

'They know this decision carries a price—your shock, the whispers of the guests, the turmoil of today. But isn't it better to pay that price now, than to see them pay a far heavier price tomorrow? Turmoil settles, but a broken bond leaves scars for life.'

~

Rohan and Sanjana had taken a step back. They reflected, they allowed silence to do its work. But they also knew they couldn't be in this state forever. The time had come to act. That's the balance life constantly demands of us—to think deeply but to then act courageously.

Some people spend their whole lives in what psychologists call analysis paralysis. They replay every possibility, weigh every risk and consult every voice, but never actually move. It feels safe to stay in the realm of thoughts. But what does that safety cost? Opportunities that are lost, relationships that fade, dreams that die quietly while we are still debating what to do.

How many times have we said that we'll start when we're ready—whether it's to do with writing that book, leaving that toxic job or admitting our feelings to someone—only to find that the perfect time never comes? Endless thinking can look like prudence, but sometimes it is simply fear dressed as wisdom.

This is Sugriva's trap in *Kishkindha Kand*, the fourth canto of the Ramayana. After Sita's abduction, when Shri Ram and Lakshman went searching for her, Hanuman brought them to Sugriva, the monkey king. When Ram asked, 'Have you seen Sita?' Sugriva said yes—he even had proof: the jewels she had dropped in her struggle. But then came the shocker: Sugriva had done nothing. He had seen, but not acted.

Now, contrast that with the behaviour of Jatayu, the noble bird. He never saw Sita with his eyes—he only heard her cries. And yet he acted instantly, throwing himself at Ravana, fighting with every feather, every ounce of strength, even giving up his life to protect her.

Sugriva thought, but did nothing. Jatayu acted, and gave everything.

One became a symbol of hesitation, the other of sacrifice. And that's the real test for all of us—we need to not only know what is right, but act on it when it matters. We must strive to not stay suspended between thought and action, and step forward with courage when life calls.

Some of us act first, think later. We jump into commitments, buy things we don't need, speak words we can't take back, enter into relationships we aren't ready for—all because pausing feels uncomfortable. Doing something, anything, feels like relief. But often that relief is temporary, and the damage lasts.

And this was Ravana's arrogance in *Yuddha Kand*, or *Lanka Kand*, the sixth canto of the Ramayana. Surrounded by sycophants who assured him, 'Monkeys and bears are our food, why think at all?', he rushed into war without reflection.

Ravana's brother Vibhishan warned him, 'Remember Hanuman. One monkey set Lanka aflame. Do not underestimate anyone.' But Ravana brushed his fears aside. No reflection, only pride.

The result? Lanka was destroyed. Haste without wisdom leads to ruin.

And then there is *Sundar Kand*, the fifth canto of the Ramayana. Why is it called 'Sundar'? Is it merely because it is beautiful? One of the reasons is because it is in the *Sundar Kand* that Hanuman achieves balance. He reflects: I must shrink my form to enter Lanka unseen. I must move at night. I must be humble, not proud. And then he acts—leaping across the ocean, setting foot in Lanka, searching with devotion and courage. His thought guides his action. His action fulfils his thought.

That's the secret:
- *Kishkindha Kand* teaches us the danger of only thinking.

- *Lanka Kand* warns us about only doing.
- *Sundar Kand* shows us the beauty of thoughtful action—wisdom married to courage.

Isn't this what we struggle with daily?

At work, how many brilliant projects never leave the whiteboard because teams debate endlessly, waiting for the 'perfect plan'? That's *Kishkindha Kand*.

And how many reckless ventures collapse because leaders rushed to launch them without listening, without reflection? That's *Lanka Kand*.

But the projects that thrive—the ones that change lives—are those where reflection matures into timely action. That's *Sundar Kand*.

Or take the case of relationships. Some people think endlessly—should I call? Should I say I'm sorry? What if they reject me?—until the relationship dies of silence. Others act rashly—send angry texts, cut ties in a moment of ego, confess love in haste—and regret it for years. But the relationships that survive are the ones where we pause to reflect, then act with honesty and courage.

But sometimes, even after all the reflection, consultation, prayer and deliberate action, some decisions will still go wrong. And that's okay. That's life. Every wrong decision, if sincere, becomes experience. Every mistake can be a stepping stone—as long as we don't confuse recklessness for courage, or endless analysis for wisdom.

There's a story that captures this well.

Someone once asked a billionaire the secret of his success.

He replied, 'Two words: right decisions.'

'And how do you make right decisions?' the man asked.

'One word: experience.'

'And how do you get experience?'

'Two words: wrong decisions.'

The lesson is simple: Success is born out of learning, not perfection—and sometimes the best teachers are the choices that didn't go as planned.

This applies not just to billionaires or boardrooms but to every one of us. Think of the career path you once chose that didn't feel right—maybe you changed lanes later, but that detour taught you resilience. Think of the friendship you held on to for too long or ended too quickly—it was painful, yes, but it taught you what kind of bond you truly want. Think of moving to a new city or saying 'yes' when you weren't sure—even if it was hard, you grew in ways you never would have otherwise.

Of course, the stakes feel higher in relationships than in office projects. These choices touch hearts, families and futures. Yet the principle still holds: Pause when needed, reflect sincerely and then act with courage. Not endless hesitation, not reckless haste—but a mindful step taken when the heart is ready.

Because in the end, life is not about avoiding wrong decisions altogether; it is about allowing even those wrong turns to become part of the wisdom that guides us forward.

So don't fear wrong decisions more than you fear indecision. If you think and never act, you will miss life. If you act and never think, you will break life. But if you think sincerely, act courageously and learn humbly, even wrong decisions help us on the path towards wisdom.

That's why Rohan and Sanjana's choice was powerful. They paused like in *Kishkindha Kand*, but they didn't get stuck. They avoided the rashness seen in *Lanka Kand*, but they didn't escape into fear. They walked the path seen in *Sundar Kand*—reflection ripening into action. Not perfect closure, not perfect clarity, but enough wisdom to take a step they could own.

∼

After I had spoken, the silence lingered thick and heavy.

Lakshmi wiped her cheeks, her fingers trembling. Her voice was less sharp, but heavy with ache. 'Swamiji ... I understand what you're saying. But how do I explain this to myself? I've dreamt of this day for years—to see my son married, to welcome Sanjana into our family as my daughter. And now? The mandap is ready, the world is waiting, and my heart is breaking.'

Rakesh looked away, his jaw clenched, his fists resting on his knees. 'Dreams can wait, Lakshmi,' he said quietly. 'But respect? That is what I fear losing. People will not ask about love or honesty. They will only whisper that our family could not see a wedding through. That will stay longer in people's memories than today's music.'

Gaurav's eyes were fixed on the floor. His voice was low but edged with frustration. 'Maybe Swamiji is right. Maybe this is wisdom. But it doesn't stop me from wondering—is there more that we're not being told? Fear, trust ... these words feel too small for such a big decision.' He looked up at Rohan and Sanjana, his gaze steady but searching. 'I want to believe you both. But I need time too.'

Priya shifted slightly, her eyes never leaving Gaurav's. Her voice was quiet but it carried a gentle firmness. 'Gauravji, sometimes the hardest truth is not about explanations but about refusing to pretend. Maybe what they've chosen doesn't make sense to us, but they are being honest with themselves. And sometimes ... that's enough.'

And then, true to herself, Dadi broke the tension with a sharp tap of her stick. '*Arré bas!* How long will we sit here crying and worrying about people's tongues? I have carefully considered everything the kids had to say. I feel it is better to delay a wedding than to rush into a divorce. If these two have the sense to pause, let us have the sense to support them.' She sniffed, straightening her dupatta with a flourish. 'And remember—this only means one thing. Another wedding feast! Haan, Priya beta, make sure the laddus are bigger next time.'

Laughter, faint and uneven, punctuated the tears. Even Lakshmi managed a weak smile through her sobs. Rakesh shook his head, muttering under his breath, but the corner of his lips twitched. Gaurav exhaled deeply, still restless but quieter.

The tension hadn't vanished, but the air felt lighter.

Rohan squeezed Sanjana's hand before speaking. 'Ma, Papa ... I know today feels like a loss. But believe me, this is not the end of our journey—it is the beginning, and we have begun with care. We are not asking you to approve our fears. We are asking you to bless our patience. If we wait, it is only because we want to come to this mandap again with hearts unshaken.'

Sanjana lifted her veil slightly, her eyes glistening as she turned to Lakshmi. 'Ma ... I still long to call you that. And I will. Today is not a rejection, it is a promise that when I walk to you again as a bride, I will carry no doubts, no hesitation, only love. Please don't think I am stepping away. I am only stepping carefully, so that I never have to step back.'

Her words touched something tender in everyone's hearts. Lakshmi pressed her hand to her mouth, fresh tears spilling over, but this time they carried not only pain but softness too. She reached out and touched Sanjana's cheek, whispering, 'Beta ...'

Even Rakesh's shoulders slumped. He rubbed his forehead and muttered, 'Hmph. You both speak like philosophers now. Just remember, philosophy doesn't feed a courtyard full of guests.' But his tone had lost its edge.

I looked at them all and said softly, 'This is what truth looks like in families—uncomfortable, unexpected, but real. You all dreamed of this day. But perhaps destiny dreamed differently. A marriage is not sacred because it is performed, it is sacred because it is prepared for. What they are choosing is not delay, but dignity. And in time, you will see it was the wiser choice.'

Gaurav wiped his tears and reached for Sanjana's hand. His voice trembled, but the words were firm. 'Fine. Maybe I don't understand everything today. But I can see this much— you both are serious. And if you are serious about making this work, then I'll stand by you. Even if I'm still restless inside.'

Lakshmi sniffed, her tears slowing. 'Yes ... if the two of you are together, and Swamiji's blessings are with you, then what more do we really need?'

Now that the mood had shifted, Priya drew in a long breath. She looked around the room—at Lakshmi's damp eyes, at Rakesh's tired shoulders, at Dadi's sharp but tender gaze—and then at Gaurav.

'Since everyone is speaking the truth today,' she said, her voice steady but her hands clasped tightly in her lap, 'perhaps I should too.'

Gaurav's head snapped towards her, alarm flashing in his eyes. 'Priya—' he began, his voice low, almost a plea, but she raised a hand gently, stopping him.

'I've carried this in my heart for too long,' she continued. 'After Vinay passed, I thought I could never feel love again. My whole life became about Ved, my work, my duties. But after meeting Gaurav … something stirred inside me. I spoke to Dadi first. She told me not to carry guilt for being human. And then I spoke to Gaurav himself. He … he listened, and he did not turn away. He said he was open to this, if I was. So yes, I must speak now—before all of you. I want to give this a chance.'

The corridor went utterly still. Gaurav shifted uneasily, eyes darting around the room, unsure about what to say.

Lakshmi was the first to react. She reached across and took Priya's hand in hers. Her voice trembled, but this time with tenderness, not shock. 'Priya … you have dealt with so much, for so long. If this brings you joy, if Gaurav makes you feel safe again, then I am only happy for you. You deserve love, beta—as much as anyone else.'

Rakesh, still blinking in surprise, let out a small laugh under his breath. 'Arré … I didn't see this coming. But if your heart is at peace, Priya, then you have our blessings too. Gaurav,' he added, glancing at him, 'look after her well. That is all I ask.'

Before anyone else could speak, there was a sound at the doorway. Ved stumbled in, looking sheepish. His ears burned red as everyone turned to him, but his voice was surprisingly clear.

'I wasn't called in,' he admitted, 'but I couldn't help listening. And honestly, I need to say something too.' He looked first at Rohan and Sanjana, a small grin tugging at his lips. 'You two ... wow. To stand here, in front of everyone, and say what you just said—that takes guts. Mama, Mami—I'm proud of you both.' He gave a mock salute that drew a few chuckles. 'Seriously, though, you showed me that honesty may shake people for a moment, but it builds respect for a lifetime.'

He turned to the rest of the room. 'And to all of you—thank you. For standing by them, and by us. Not every family does this. Some run away from the truth. This family ... you leaned in. I'm proud to be a part of it. Even if sometimes you all argue like you are in a web-series family drama.'

We all laughed.

Then Ved shifted closer to Gaurav, his expression softening. 'And now ... my turn. It might take me some time to stop saying "Gaurav Uncle" and start saying "Dad". But I want to. Because I love him. He's been wonderful to me—always friendly, helpful, kind, supportive ... and most importantly, funny. He makes me feel like I have someone who's got my back. And I want that. We want that.'

For a moment, no one moved. Ved's words had settled in the air like a blessing—gentle, disarming, impossible to ignore.

Lakshmi's tears had returned, but this time they flowed with relief. She reached out, pulling Ved into her arms, her voice quivering. 'Beta ... after everything, to hear you speak like this ... You've made me believe again. Your papa would have been so proud.' She kissed the top of his head.

Rakesh cleared his throat, blinking faster than usual to hide his watery eyes, though he tried to disguise it as irritation. 'Arré, this boy,' he muttered, shaking his head, 'he just stole the spotlight from the dulha and dulhan.' But the smile that broke across his face betrayed him. 'Ved, I'm proud of you. If you can accept Gaurav so openly, then who are we to hold back?'

Gaurav swallowed hard, his composure visibly crumbling. He pulled Ved closer, hugging him tightly. His voice cracked as he whispered, 'You've no idea how much this means, champ. I was nervous about all of this ... but you just made me feel at home. You ... you made me belong.'

Priya stood close beside them, wiping her tears with the back of her hand. She placed her palm over Gaurav and Ved's clasped hands, and said in a trembling voice, 'This is all I ever wanted—for us to be whole. Not perfect, but whole.'

Rohan and Sanjana exchanged a glance, surprise flickering into warmth. Rohan smiled faintly. 'Well, I suppose if today is about honesty, then this was the right time.'

Sanjana nodded, her eyes soft. 'Yes. Love doesn't always arrive the way we plan it—but arrive it does.'

Dadi slapped her knee with her palm, grinning from ear to ear. 'Wah! This corridor has turned into a confession box. Good! Better to pour it all out here than to carry it inside like poison. Priya, beta, you have my blessings. Gaurav, you already had my suspicion, now you have my approval too!' She winked at Ved. 'And you—today you spoke like a saint but joked like me. Clearly, my genes.'

Laughter erupted, and the air became lighter than it had been all day.

The corridor, which only an hour ago had felt like the eye of a storm, now vibrated with warmth. Tears had turned into blessings, tension into laughter. What remained was not perfection but truth—and in that truth, the family felt whole.

Rakesh sat back on one of the chairs in the corridor, sinking into his seat as the weight of the day pressed into him. He let out a long sigh, then nodded slowly, as though he had reached the edge of his resistance and found a measure of calm there.

'Fine,' he said at last. 'Let the guests eat, let the band play. We will celebrate anyway. Today will still be remembered. Yes, we did not go ahead with the rituals but we passed the test of this family's strength and love for each other.' He paused, then turned towards me. 'But Swamiji ... I have a request. Don't let this be whispered in corners, passed like gossip from one ear to another. Tell everyone. Spread the news freely. Not like an announcement, but like a wedding speech. With humour, with heart. Let them laugh with us, feel with us, and understand. If the script has changed, let it change in the open.'

∼

The courtyard buzzed with laughter and chatter, the band still playing, the air rich with the fragrance of marigolds and incense. Guests waited expectantly, some restless, some whispering about the delay.

At last, Rakesh stepped forward, his face composed but his eyes carrying the weight of what had just unfolded. Grabbing the microphone, he lifted a hand to quiet the murmurs.

'Dear friends, thank you so much for your patience,' he began, his voice steady, carrying over the sound of the receding dhols. 'The muhurat is soon approaching ... but before that, we realized something. In all the joy of the sangeet, the colour of the mehendi, the laughter of the haldi—what we missed out on was Swamiji's words of blessing and wisdom. The wedding speech.'

A ripple of murmurs and nods swept through the crowd, the anticipation shifting into curiosity.

Rakesh continued, his tone softening, 'My family and I are truly honoured to have him in our lives—not only as a guest here today, but as a friend, philosopher and guide. And today, in this moment, I want you all to hear him too, and be inspired as we have been. So ladies and gentlemen, I will hand over the microphone now ... Swamiji, the stage is all yours.'

He extended the mic towards me, his hand lingering for a moment, as though passing not just the microphone but the weight of the truth that needed to be carried.

I took the microphone, smiling at the sea of expectant faces.

'A very good afternoon to you, ladies and gentlemen. Thank you so much, Rakeshji, for those kind words. Though, to be honest, whenever someone introduces me as a "friend, philosopher and guide", I wonder if I should just start charging consulting fees. Monk perks, you know.'

Laughter rippled through the crowd.

'Friends, what a wonderful couple of days we've had together. The sangeet gave us music and dance, and I must say, I've never seen so many people perform moves that would give any Bollywood choreographer a complex. Honestly, half of those steps haven't even been invented yet.'

The audience chuckled, some teasing each other already. Rakesh, despite the intensity of the earlier moments, shook his head with a smile.

'And then the mehendi—such beautiful patterns painted on people's hands, each one a story. The only problem is, once the mehendi is on, the ladies can't use their hands. Which is why all the men were suddenly promoted to "temporary assistants"—holding purses, answering phones, even feeding pani puris one by one to their better halves.'

The crowd laughed louder, a few men nodding knowingly. Lakshmi, still teary-eyed from earlier, found herself chuckling too, nudging a cousin beside her.

'Then there was the haldi … ah, the haldi. Well, the less I say about that battlefield, the better. But the walls of this palace are now brighter than the sun.

'And now, after all that singing, dancing, painting, we are finally here—the grand finale, the wedding day, waiting for the pheras. Weddings, you know, are not just rituals … they're full-time degree programmes.'

I paused, letting curiosity spread through the courtyard. Ved leaned forward, eager for what was coming next.

'Yes! This is the day when the man officially loses his bachelor's degree … and the woman gets her master's.'

The courtyard erupted with laughter, the men groaning good-naturedly, the women clapping and cheering. Even Sanjana, her veil still framing her thoughtful eyes, let out a soft laugh.

'How many of you married men here agree?' I asked, raising my hand.

Most of the men, smiling sheepishly, raised their hands, while the ladies cheered even louder.

Lowering my voice, I said, 'And the men who didn't raise their hands ... were silently nudged by their wives not to.'

That elicited another round of laughter, playful teasing bouncing across the courtyard. I smiled and let the laughter run its course, then waited for the quiet to return.

'But jokes apart, friends—beneath all the colour, music and teasing lies the real heart of a wedding. A wedding is not just about one big day. It is about all the ordinary days that follow. It is not about the fireworks of the sangeet, or the beauty of the mehendi or even the fun of the haldi. It is about whether, in the quiet of everyday life, two people can still laugh together, still listen to each other, still carry each other's burdens.'

The courtyard had grown quieter now, the smiles softer, more thoughtful.

'A wedding is not a destination—it is a beginning. The pheras, the vows, the rituals—they are not certificates that guarantee happiness. They are reminders, like signposts, that the journey ahead must be built with patience, forgiveness and love. Because in the end, marriage is less about finding the right person and more about becoming the right partner.'

I paused and scanned the crowd. 'How many of you here have ever baked a cake?'

Hands went up, laughter bubbled in pockets amongst the audience.

'Ah, then, you know that baking a cake takes patience. You can't just crank up the oven and hope the cake bakes faster. If you do that, it burns on the outside and stays raw on the inside.

And isn't that just like how it is with relationships? They can't be rushed. They need time, consistency and the right balance of ingredients. Too much ego, too little communication, one spoonful of anger extra—and the cake flops.'

The crowd chuckled, with some people eyeing their partners playfully.

'Once the cake is nicely baking, then comes the icing. Now, the icing gives the cake its delicious taste and beautiful look. But here's the thing—if the icing's too runny, it'll slide right off, no matter how great the cake is. Romance is like that—lovely to look at, wonderful to taste, but it only stays when it's steady.

'And then of course, there's the famous "cherry on top". That little decoration that makes everyone say "Wow!" The cherry is like all the extras in life—the destination weddings, the designer outfits, the fancy Instagram reels. Lovely to have, but remember—if the cake is bad, no cherry can save it. You can post the best photos online, but offline, you'll be stuck eating something inedible.'

The guests laughed louder now, clapping at the analogy.

'If the icing and the cherry are a bit off, but the cake is baked well—you can still enjoy it. Because the cake is the foundation. The real substance. Similarly, wedding rituals are all like the icing and the cherry. Fun, beautiful, sacred, necessary—but they do not make the marriage itself. What really matters is the cake—the bond, the commitment, the trust between two people. If that's not right, life ahead becomes a problem.'

I paused for effect, then added with a smile, 'I once met a lady who was wearing her wedding ring on the wrong finger. I asked her why. She replied, "Because I married the wrong guy."'

The crowd laughed, while a knowing murmur of agreement rippled through the elders.

'And that, my friends, is why baking the cake properly is critical. Because no amount of decoration can save a cake that is raw inside. And no amount of rituals, flowers or music can save a marriage that isn't ready on the inside.'

I let the words settle, then softened my tone.

'Today, Rohan and Sanjana reminded us of this very truth. They stood at the edge of the mandap, with the world watching, and realized that the cake is still baking. The ingredients are all there—love, care, friendship, trust. But it needs more time in the oven of life. And they had the courage to say, "Let's not rush. Let's not serve half-baked promises. Let's wait until we are ready to honour the vows fully."'

The courtyard grew still. The guests glanced at each other, some surprised, some confused. Rakesh exhaled slowly, and the tension seemed to seep out of him. Sanjana looked at Rohan with tears that shimmered with relief, not shame.

'Now, I know some of you might have expected to see the icing today—the rituals, the pheras, the fire. But tell me, would you rather have a beautiful-looking cake that tastes miserable, or a cake that's baked to perfection, even if the icing comes a little later? That is what Rohan and Sanjana chose. Not to cancel love, but to strengthen it. Not to run away from each other, but to walk more carefully towards each other.'

I smiled gently.

'Better to pause now than regret later. Better to wait with honesty than proceed with pretence. That is not weakness—it is wisdom.'

The crowd, which had been holding its breath, began to nod, the silence more accepting.

'And trust me, there are absolutely no issues between the two of them. Nothing is wrong. They didn't realize until yesterday that they both needed more time before the icing and the cherry. And honestly, isn't that what life teaches us? Sometimes you only discover in the quiet moments what you couldn't see in the noise of celebration. That pause, that honesty is their strength.'

I let the words rest a moment before continuing. Gaurav, seated quietly, nodded at last, his apprehensions giving way to understanding.

'But the beauty of today is this—it wasn't just Rohan and Sanjana who chose honesty. This whole family decided that today would not just be a wedding day, but a day of truth.

'So you see, my friends, this day has given us more than the promise of rituals. It has given us truths. Love spoken honestly, bonds embraced openly, courage shown quietly. And that, I dare say, is worth celebrating even more than a set of pheras done in haste.

'Sometimes I joke that marriage is like a pack of cards— it begins with diamonds and hearts but often ends with clubs and spades. But I believe it should be the other way round. Better to be faced with clubs and spades first—the disagreements, the differences, the clashes. And by working through them, you reach the diamonds and hearts.

'Because the real test of love is not how sweetly it begins, but how strongly it survives through the seasons. Hearts matter, diamonds matter—but they shine the brightest only after the clubs and spades have done their work.

'Rohan and Sanjana may not have faced all their clubs and spades yet, but I am sure they will. And when they do, may they be led to more diamonds, more hearts and more joy. Because that, in the end, is the winning hand.'

I let the murmurs of agreement and the nods echo through the courtyard before lowering my voice.

I turned towards the priests and the family. 'Today is still as auspicious as it was meant to be. The muhurat has begun. Let the yajna be lit. Let Sanjana and Rohan vow to return when they are ready. In fact, let us all walk around that fire, in silence, in our hearts, and secretly, but honestly, take our own vows.'

I paused. 'So let us celebrate. Let the dhols play louder, let the grand feast be served and let us remember that love has not been delayed, it has only been made more real.'

People broke into applause—not the polite kind that is offered when one is lightly impressed, but a heartfelt standing ovation, the kind that comes only when people are moved, when they feel they've witnessed something true. Laughter mingled with tears, and the heaviness dissolved into joy. The band struck up again, louder than before, and the wedding that might have been remembered as incomplete was instead remembered as unforgettable.

∽

And perhaps, dear reader, that is the invitation for all of us. We may not always stand before a sacred fire in a palace courtyard, but each of us has our own yajnas—those moments when life forces us to pause and asks: What truly matters now?

Sometimes it is the courage to close a door, and at other times it is the humility to open one. Sometimes it is the discipline to persist, sometimes it is the wisdom to pause. These quiet yajnas are not marked by mantras, but by the decisions we make when no one is watching. It is those choices, repeated with integrity, that slowly turn the ordinary into the sacred.

The family stood together—Rakesh and Lakshmi side by side, their eyes still moist but their faces bright with pride; Rohan and Sanjana close to each other, fingers entwined, their expressions carrying both relief and resolve; Priya, leaning ever so slightly towards Gaurav, with Ved wedged happily between them; and Dadi, stick in hand, grinning wider than anyone, her presence tying them all together with the invisible thread of blessings.

For a moment, beneath the marigolds and the music, they were more than just a family. They were a picture of love—imperfect, unfinished but honest—and that honesty had made them whole. Yet becoming whole is never the end of a story, only the beginning of a life waiting to be lived.

....

THINGS TO THINK ABOUT ...

ALIGNING THOUGHT AND ACTION:
- Kishkindha Kand = Endless thinking without action → Stagnation.
- Lanka Kand = Reckless action without reflection → Destruction.
- Sundar Kand = Beauty lies in balance: Thoughtful reflection + courageous action.
- Wrong decisions teach lessons. The real failure lies in indecision.
- In work, relationships and personal life, wisdom is not in thinking or doing, but in aligning the two.

MARRIAGE IS A BEGINNING: Pheras and vows are not guarantees of happiness but reminders that marriage is a journey to be built daily, in ordinary moments of listening, laughing and carrying each other's burdens.

A GOOD CAKE NEEDS TIME TO BAKE:
- A relationship, like a cake, needs time to bake. Rushing leaves it raw inside.
- Romance is the icing—sweet but only steady if the base is strong.
- The extras—designer outfits, destination weddings, Instagram reels—are the cherries. Lovely, but they can't save a badly baked cake.

UNIVERSAL VOWS: Marriage is a reminder for everyone—not just the bride and groom—to reflect, to silently take their vows in their own hearts: to be patient, to forgive, to love more deeply.

•••••••••••••••

The exercises related to the concepts mentioned in this chapter can be found on p. 284.

11

A Monk at the Mandap

Can We Have It All?

~

The story isn't over when the crowd disperses—it continues quietly in the choices we carry forward.

The evening of the wedding day lingered like incense—fragrant to some, irritating to others, eliciting different reactions in every corner it reached.

Some guests admired the decision deeply. They whispered to one another that it took real courage to stop at the mandap rather than going ahead with the rituals for the sake of performing for society. To them, it was not a wedding delayed, but wisdom revealed. A few others, though, sat firmly on the fence. 'Yes, honesty is good,' they muttered over desserts, 'but couldn't they have thought of this earlier? Why wait till the mandap?' Their heads were sympathetic while their hearts wrestled with doubt.

Some were openly disapproving. 'What will people say?' they sighed, shaking their heads. For them, reputation outweighed reflection. The spectacle of a mandap left unused was more outrageous to their minds than the quiet dignity of two people choosing the truth.

Then there were those for whom it hardly mattered. As long as it didn't affect their own lives, they were fine with anything anyone chose to do. Live and let live—provided it required nothing of them. And of course, there were always some who found in the events of the day the perfect spice for gossip—something to dissect, exaggerate and retell long after the band had packed up. For them, what really happened wasn't important, the story they could spin out of it was.

The truth is people rarely see things as they are. They see them as *they* are. Their lens becomes their world. Don't they say: There is my story, there is their story and then there is the story. And even 'the story', the so-called objective truth, is never untouched. It is flavoured by our biases, filtered by our experiences and spun by our imagination.

So should it matter at all? The answer depends on what we value more—applause outside or alignment inside. Because applause comes and goes, but alignment stays. One fills the ear, the other fills the heart.

∽

The night wound down, the fairy lights dimmed and the petals that lay scattered across the courtyard curled at their edges. The dhols too fell silent, and the palace that had thundered with the sounds of merriment and the storm of unexpected decisions now slipped into silence. Yet the echo of that decision—brave to some, baffling to others—lingered like a refrain.

And then came the morning after.

The palace stirred awake differently that day. Not with trumpets or drone cameras, but with the softer rhythm of recuperation. This was day 3.5 of the wedding—when everyone had to sport the much-anticipated 'Recovery Casual' looks.

After three and a half days of sequins, selfies, sherwanis and buffets, the vibe was finally different. Pyjamas replaced lehengas, sneakers replaced juttis. The fragrance of incense gave way to the sharp comfort of strong ginger chai. Guests lounged under canopies in loose kurtas, sunglasses shielding their tired eyes, while waiters carried trays of tender coconut water, lemon soda and steaming samosas that disappeared faster than they appeared.

For some, the previous night's decision was still the subject of hushed conversations. For others, it was already yesterday's news. But for the family, for those who had stood in that corridor and heard the truth first-hand, the morning felt different. It wasn't just recovery from three days of celebration, they were arising from a night that had shaken hearts and tested love, yet left behind the quiet strength of courage.

After my morning chanting and sadhana, I sat in my suite with my notebook open, the palace finally quiet in a way it hadn't been for days. I wanted to capture my thoughts before I said goodbye. And as I wrote, I realized that what I had witnessed in these three and a half days was not just a wedding, but life itself—distilled into moments, lessons and truths.

Those lessons became the ten principles I shared with you in the form of the ten chapters before this. Not as theories, but as living wisdom drawn from stories, rituals, tears, laughter and the courage of people who chose to be real.

Isn't it true, friends, that whether in our relationships, our work or our spiritual life, we all want to 'have it all'? To make life perfect and complete before it is finished?

A married man at the wedding joked: 'What's the difference between complete and finished? If you find the right life partner, life is complete. If you find the wrong one, life is finished. And if the right one catches you with the wrong one, then life is completely finished!'

Everyone had laughed, and I had joined in as well. But humour aside, isn't this how we often approach life? As if it were a perfect platter where every dish must be placed just right before we can enjoy it? But life rarely serves us our meals that way.

Life is more like a home-cooked meal—sometimes a dish is missing, sometimes the salt is less, sometimes the food turns out to be too spicy and sometimes the dal accidentally spills into the curry. And yet, if we choose to savour it, even the imperfections are bursting with flavour. The food may not look picture-perfect, but it can still nourish, surprise and delight us. Especially when it's cooked with love—like a mother's meal, where the taste lies less in the perfection and more in the affection.

So can we have it all? Maybe yes, maybe no.

If by 'all' we mean perfection, control, guarantees—then no. That 'all' is an illusion. Life will always hand us cracks, delays, misunderstandings, conflicts, failures and snakes when we expected ladders.

But if by 'all' we mean something deeper—growth, connection, harmony, peace, happiness, purpose, love—then yes, we can have it *all*. Not because life neatly serves it to us, but because we can learn to get there.

And here are the ten principles to unlock a fuller life:

1. **Understanding:** When we understand ourselves, we find peace. When we understand others, we find harmony. When we understand our calling, we find purpose.
2. **Manifestation:** When we cultivate resilience, sincerity, patience and values, we build a garden where the butterflies of success, love and peace naturally land.
3. **Acceptance:** When we accept our imperfections while still aspiring to grow, we unlock peace and self-worth.
4. **Transformation:** When we rise above bitterness through wisdom, support, small joys and acts of service, we find betterness—a life that feels lighter and richer.
5. **Balance:** When we align our duties with our desires, weaving responsibility with passion, we move forward without neglecting either.

6. **Foundation:** When trust, respect, communication, values and commitment are in place, relationships endure. When we shift our inner energy, the right people and opportunities arrive.
7. **Communication:** When we replace assumptions with conversations, trust is restored, both in love and in work.
8. **Vulnerability:** When we drop our masks and allow ourselves to be seen—or at least be honest with ourselves and God—we discover authenticity.
9. **Maturity:** When decisions are not made in haste or fear, but through pause and reflection, we grow in wisdom and strength.
10. **Alignment:** When thought and action walk together—neither frozen in endless reflection, nor reckless in blind haste—we find growth, experience and meaning.

And perhaps most importantly, beyond all these principles, we unlock a better life when we stop showing trailers to the world and start living the full movie—raw, messy and unfinished, but real.

That, to me, is having it all. Not a life without cracks, but a life where the cracks don't break us. Not a life without storms, but a life where storms teach us to bend and still stand tall. Not a life that looks perfect in photos, but a life that feels authentic when no one is watching.

So no, life will never be 'complete' in the ways we imagine. But it can be whole. And wholeness, I've come to believe, is better.

By late afternoon, the grand lobby, which only days ago had looked like the red-carpet entrance of a film premiere, was now filled with suitcases rolling across marble floors, children clutching leftover balloons and aunties carefully packing away extra boxes of laddus 'for the journey'.

The family stood under the main archway, a line of smiles and folded hands, seeing everyone off as though the rituals of farewell were as sacred as those of welcome. Lakshmi's eyes brimmed again with tears as she hugged relatives who had travelled from afar. Rakesh, ever the gracious host, insisted that every departing guest carry both blessings and snacks, saying with half a smile, 'One for the road, one for the memories.'

And there, still at the entrance, stood the life-size cutout of the bride and groom—their faces glowing with the thrill of new beginnings. When the guests had first arrived, they had paused to click selfies with it, a fun teaser for the celebrations to come. Now, however, after all that had unfolded, I couldn't help but think: Trailers set expectations, yet the real story is always more layered, more human, more raw than any poster can ever capture.

And isn't life a little like that too? We put out our trailers—the highlights on social media, the polished introductions, the smiling photographs. But underneath them lies the full movie, with all its edits and retakes, its unplanned twists and unscripted truths. The world may applaud the trailer, but it is only in living the story—in all its messiness and depth—that true meaning is found.

Some guests left quickly, chauffeured cars whisking them away to the airport. Others lingered, reluctant to be released from the palace's spell. They paused for selfies under the archways, strolled once more through the courtyard, as if trying to bottle up the last drops of festivity. The photographers had packed up, the planners looked drained, yet the fragrance of flowers still hung faintly in the air, as though the palace itself was reluctant to let go.

Children waved from car windows, their voices trailing off in sing-song goodbyes. Friends and cousins shouted promises of reunions, though everyone knew they'd probably meet next at another wedding. Slowly, the palace emptied.

And then it was my turn.

I had stood quietly at the back, watching the stream of people departing, letting the warmth of embraces and the tenderness of farewells wash over me.

My small strolley had been brought down by the staff, but I insisted on carrying it myself to the car this time.

The family stood together—as if the farewell itself were another ritual.

Lakshmi stepped forward first, joining her palms in namaste, her eyes wet but peaceful. 'Swamiji,' she said softly, 'thank you … for being here, for holding us together through yesterday.'

I returned the gesture. 'You were all fine on your own,' I said. 'I only held the umbrella when the clouds arrived.' Her lips curved into a faint smile, the kind that comes when tears have finally run their course.

Rakesh clasped me in a quick, earnest hug—the dignified sort that men give when they don't want to cry. His voice caught slightly. 'You turned a difficult day into a meaningful one.'

I chuckled, patting his shoulder. 'And you reminded me that sometimes even serious hosts know how to laugh.'

He laughed, the weight of the previous day finally lifting. 'One for the road, one for the memories,' he said, slipping a box of sweets into my bag like contraband affection.

Dadi lifted her hand and placed it firmly on my head, her palm warm with years of love and strength. 'Arré, monk sahib,' she said, grinning, her eyes twinkling, 'you gave a blockbuster speech without a single item song. Next time— no escaping—I want at least one line dedicated only to grandmothers.'

I bowed theatrically. 'Done, Dadi. The chorus is yours.'

She raised her stick like a conductor's baton, smiling as if she had just won the argument for all grandmothers everywhere.

Priya stepped forward next, her smile tender, steady. 'Thank you,' she said simply, placing her hand over her heart. 'For helping us tell the truth.' Gaurav stood beside her, awkward and grateful. 'And for making "funny" an official requirement,' he added.

'The most sacred vows,' I said, 'are the ones that make you laugh on the inside.'

Rohan and Sanjana came last, their fingers entwined. 'You gave us the words we didn't have to express ourselves,' Rohan said quietly. 'And you gave us time,' Sanjana added, 'without making us feel small for asking.'

I joined my palms together. 'You gave yourselves those gifts. I only held the mirror for you.'

I was about to turn when Ved jogged up to me, slightly breathless, wearing a hoodie despite the desert warmth. 'Gaurji—wait.' He reached into his tote, pulled out a brown kraft envelope and handed it to me with a grin that tried very hard to disguise his nervousness.

Inside was a charcoal sketch. It was a depiction of the mandap: the yajna flames lifting up like quiet tongues of light, and at the microphone—me, my robe flowing into lines that became garlands, that became hands joined in namaste all across the page. At the bottom, he had scrawled a title: 'A Monk at the Mandap'.

For a moment, my eyes stung.

'Ved,' I said softly, 'you've done what the best cameras can't. You've managed to capture the feeling.'

'Gaurji,' he said, suddenly shy, 'thank you for ... for seeing me. Like, actually seeing me.'

I looked down at the sketch. 'And thank you for showing me what can't always be said in words,' I replied. 'Like, actually showing.'

'Also,' he added, twirling a set of car keys, 'Nanu asked if I could drop you to the airport, like I picked you up. Your chariot awaits, Gaurji.'

Outside, the afternoon sun poured gold over the sandstone walls of the palace. The same black S-Class idled at the curb. The chauffeur reached for my bag, but Ved shook his head, tucked the sketch back into its envelope, picked up my bag and opened the rear door with a flourish. 'After you, Monk Boss.'

I raised an eyebrow. 'Servant Guy,' I corrected.

He grinned. 'Right. Servant Boss.'

∼

As I walked towards security, I tucked Ved's sketch into my bag, feeling its gentle weight. Outside, somewhere beyond the airport's glass facade, a nineteen-year-old in an oversized hoodie and sneakers was getting into a car, feeling a bit better than he had yesterday. And inside the airport, beneath his saffron robe, a monk too walked a little lighter—not from speaking his heart, but from being trusted to listen.

And that, I think, my friends, is how you can have it all—not by holding everything, but by holding the right things close: love, truth, laughter … and the courage to live them to their fullest.

....

THINGS TO THINK ABOUT …

PEOPLE RARELY SEE THINGS AS THEY ARE: They see them through the lens of who they are. Every story is shaped by perspective—my story, their story and the story—and each is coloured by bias, memory and emotion. The real question isn't how the world sees us, but what we hold sacred—the noise of applause or the quiet of integrity. Applause fades, inner steadiness lasts. One echoes outside, the other rests within.

HAVING IT ALL:
- If 'having it all' means having a flawless life where everything goes as planned, without cracks or chaos, then no, it doesn't exist.
- Life will always surprise us with its detours and imperfections.
- But if 'having it all' means finding growth, love, peace and meaning within those imperfections, then yes, we can have it all. Not because life is perfect, but because we learn to live fully and grow gently within its imperfections.

THE TEN KEYS TO UNLOCK A FULLER LIFE:
1. Understanding
2. Manifestation
3. Acceptance
4. Transformation
5. Balance
6. Foundation
7. Communication
8. Vulnerability
9. Maturity
10. Alignment

••••••••••••••

The exercises related to the concepts mentioned in this chapter can be found on p. 290.

Your Thought Journal

Monkify

CHAPTER 1

Worksheet 1.1: Practising Understanding over Agreement

Part 1: Awareness

Recall a recent situation where you strongly disagreed with someone. What was the issue?

Work example: A senior teammate preferred following the usual process, while I wanted to try a new approach to improve efficiency.

Home example: My partner wanted to spend the weekend with friends, while I wanted quiet time together at home.

Generational example: My parents wanted me to take up a 'secure' government job, while I wanted to pursue a start-up idea.

👍 _____
_____
_____

What was your perspective?

👍 _____
_____
_____

What was theirs?

👍 _____
_____
_____

Part 2: Reflection Prompts

What emotions came up for you in that moment?

👍 _____
_____
_____

What human need might the other person have been trying to express?

✍ _____
_____
_____

Looking back, what mattered more—being right or staying connected?

✍ _____
_____
_____

Part 3: Shifts in Perspective

Write one sentence that captures your truth in that situation.

Work example: A report should be clear and straightforward.

Home example: We need weekends to nurture our relationship.

Generational example: I need to give my dreams a shot while I still have the energy.

✍ _____
_____
_____

Write one sentence that might capture their truth.

Work example: A report should also capture attention and stand out.

Home example: Friendships also need time and care.

Generational example: A stable job protects you from risk and hardships.

✍ _____
_____
_____

Compare the two sentences you have written down, which capture the reader and the other party's truths in the given situation.

What is overlapping?

Work example: We both wanted the report to make an impact.
Home example: We both wanted to nurture important relationships.
Generational example: My parents and I want my life to be meaningful and successful.

👉 _____
_____
_____

Where is the gap?

Work example: Different methods—clarity vs creativity.
Home example: Different focus—couple time vs friends time.
Generational example: Different definitions—security vs exploration.

👉 _____
_____
_____

Part 4: Steps to Practise

Pause before reacting: Next time I will …

Work example: Take a breath before dismissing their idea.
Home example: Take a pause before assuming I'm not a priority.
Generational example: Take a step back before getting defensive with my parents.

👉 _____
_____
_____

Ask one clarifying question: Can you explain …

Work example: 'Why do visuals matter so much to you?'

Home example: 'Why is this gathering important for you right now?'

Generational example: 'What worries you most about me choosing a start-up?'

👆 _____

_____

_____

Name the common need: We both value …

Work example: Helping the audience understand and remember the message.

Home example: Strengthening the relationships that matter to us.

Generational example: Building a secure and meaningful future.

👆 _____

_____

_____

Practise empathy: I can see that for them …

Work example: Design is a part of communication, not just decoration.

Home example: Time with friends is also a way to feel fulfilled and balanced.

Generational example: Stability is a way to show love and ensure I'm safe.

👆 _____

_____

_____

Choose connection over winning: I should remind myself that …

Work example: Understanding is more important than proving who's right.

Home example: Love grows when I respect their needs as well as mine.

Generational example: Respect builds bridges even when paths differ.

👍 _____

_____

_____

Part 5: Commitment

Write about one small action that you can take this week to practise understanding someone else's perspective.

Work example: I'll ask one clarifying question before jumping into a disagreement.

Home example: I'll listen first and suggest a compromise rather than shutting the idea down.

Generational example: With my parents, I'll acknowledge their concerns before explaining my choices.

👍 _____

_____

_____

∾

Worksheet 1.2: Pause – Reflect – Experiment

Part 1: Awareness

When do you usually feel most at peace?

Example: When I go for a quiet morning walk without my phone.

👍 _____

_____

_____

Your Thought Journal

When do you usually feel drained?

Example: Endless late-night doomscrolling leaves me tired and anxious.

✍ _____
_____
_____

When do you usually feel excited and alive?

Example: When I'm teaching or sharing ideas with friends.

✍ _____
_____
_____

Part 2: Reflection

Looking at your answers, what do you think you really need more of?

Example: I need more quiet, screen-free time.

✍ _____
_____
_____

What do you need to reduce or let go of?

Example: I need to cut back on mindless doomscrolling at night.

✍ _____
_____
_____

Part 3: Steps to Practise

Pause: Create one daily moment of stillness (5–10 minutes).

Example: I'll sit quietly for 5 minutes before bed instead of checking my phone.

✍ _____
_____
_____

Reflect: Journal your triggers, joys and drains weekly.

Example: Every night, I'll write one line in my journal about what gave me energy and what drained me during the day.

✍ _____
_____
_____

Experiment: Try one new habit/practice and notice how it feels.

Example: Replaced 10 minutes of scrolling with reading. Felt calmer and slept better.

✍ _____
_____
_____

∼

WORKSHEET 1.3: THE LITMUS TEST OF AUTHENTICITY

PART 1: RECALL AN ACTIVITY, GOAL OR DREAM

Write down something you're currently pursuing or considering pursuing.

✍ _____

PART 2: APPLY THE THREE CHECKS

Energy Check

- Does this energize me or drain me?
- Even when it's tough, does it feel meaningful?

✍ _____

Endurance Check

- Does my interest deepen the more I explore it?
- Or is it just a passing trend or hype?

✍ _____

Inner-Approval Check
- Would I still do this if nobody noticed?
- If there were no likes, applause or external validation, would it still feel worthwhile?

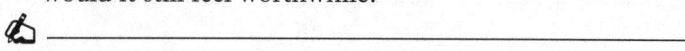

PART 3: YOUR VERDICT

After reflecting on all three checks, read the statements given below and circle one that feels true for you:

☑ This feels authentic and truly mine.

⚠ I need to reflect more before committing.

✘ This may not be authentic—it feels more like imitation.

BONUS REFLECTION

Fill in the blanks below in a way that sums up what you've learned about yourself.

✍ 'I now see that my hunger is _____, and my courageous foolishness is _____.'

CHAPTER 2

WORKSHEET 2.1: THE THREE STEPS OF NISHKAMA KARMA YOGA

PART 1: EFFORT (GIVE YOUR BEST)

Instead of asking whether life is giving you enough, ask whether *you* are showing up fully. This step is about bringing your energy, focus and sincerity into the present moment—with no comparisons, no shortcuts.

Reflection Prompt: Where, today, can I show up with more sincerity, attention or discipline than I usually do?

My effort today will be:

👍 _____

Part 2: Detachment (Release the Outcome)

You can only control your effort, not the result. Detachment doesn't mean you don't care—it means you don't let the results define your peace. It's an inner shift: from 'What will I get?' to 'What is this teaching me?'

Reflection Prompt: Which result am I overthinking, and what would it feel like to breathe and let it be?

One outcome I will release today:

👍 _____

Part 3: Service (Tie It to Something Higher)

Actions feel lighter when they are not only for 'me'. Service can be quiet, simple and woven into daily life—by offering your work with sincerity, helping someone without expecting anything back and adding value in the small moments.

Reflection Prompt: Who can benefit from my actions today—even in a small, unseen way?

One way I will serve through my action today:

👍 _____
_____
_____

Key Insight

Give with full effort. Release with detachment. Offer with love. That is Nishkama Karma Yoga.

CHAPTER 3

Worksheet 3.1: Kintsugi and Wabi-Sabi for Everyday Life

Part 1: Notice Your Cracks (Kintsugi Practice)

We all have fractures, both visible and invisible. Instead of hiding them, what if we honoured them?

What part of my body carries a scar or a mark, and what story does it tell?

✍ _____
_____
_____

What memory or experience broke me but also shaped me?

✍ _____
_____
_____

Where in my life do I feel 'less than'—and how can I see that as a source of depth, not deficiency?

✍ _____
_____
_____

Part 2: Celebrate the Ordinary (Wabi-Sabi Practice)

Wabi-Sabi is about beauty in imperfection, impermanence and incompleteness.

What is one ordinary object in my home (like a chipped plate, an old dupatta or a faded photo) that carries a memory?

✍ _____
_____
_____

What everyday moment brings quiet joy when I pause to notice it?

✍ _____
_____
_____

Where am I chasing 'perfect'—and missing the beauty of 'enough'?

✍ _____
_____
_____

Part 3: Small Shifts, Golden Light

Kintsugi and Wabi-Sabi aren't about giving up on growth—they're about shifting how we see.

One way I can wear my 'crack' with pride this week:

✍ _____
_____
_____

One small practice of acceptance I want to bring into my daily life:

✍ _____
_____
_____

One area where I'll still strive to grow—but gently, not harshly:

✍ _____
_____
_____

Part 4: Reflection Affirmation

'I am not defined by my cracks, but by the warmth I still hold.'

CHAPTER 4

WORKSHEET 4.1: MASTERING LIFE'S UNFAIR MOMENTS—WHEN TO ACCEPT, WHEN TO ACT

LIFE IS UNFAIR
GET USED TO IT
LEARN TO NEGOTIATE

In *difficult situations, what can be changed?*

ACCEPTANCE	NEGOTIATION
List the aspects of the situation that cannot be changed:	List the aspects of the situation that you can influence:
✍ _____	✍ _____
_____	_____
_____	_____
_____	_____

Wisdom lies in knowing the difference.

∼

WORKSHEET 4.2: THE FARMER'S WISDOM—WHAT'S IN MY CONTROL?

'Do your duty sincerely, without attachment to the results'
—Bhagavad Gita

PART 1: IDENTIFY YOUR 'FIELD'

What area of life are you trying to improve in or are feeling stuck in?

Example: Career/Relationship/Health/Work project/Spiritual growth

✍ My Field: _____

Part 2: The Five Factors of the Farmer's Frame

Factor	Meaning	My Reflection
1. Land (Foundation)	The situation or starting point you've been given, like your current environment or conditions.	
2. Skill (Knowledge and Discipline)	The tools and understanding you bring, like your learning, experience and attitude.	
3. Resources (Support and Tools)	The external help, materials or opportunities available to you.	
4. Effort (Action and Perseverance)	The consistent work you're putting in daily, your commitment, patience and practice.	
5. Rain (Grace and Destiny)	The factors beyond your control, like timing, luck, others' decisions, divine will, etc.	

Part 3: Circle of Control

Draw two circles in the space given below:
- In the inner circle, write what you can control (your thoughts, actions, responses).

- In the outer circle, write what you cannot control (others' opinions, outcomes, the timing).

(Tip: You can't predict the rain, but you can still prepare the soil.)

Part 4: Reflection Prompts

What am I focusing too much on—the soil or the rain?

✍ _____

_____

_____

What can I start doing today with what's already in my hands?

✍ _____

_____

_____

Where can I let go and trust the process?

✍ _____

_____

_____

Key Insight

Stop chasing what's missing. Start with what's in your hand. Till the soil. Sow the seeds. Let the rains—when they come—be a gift, not a guarantee.

∼

CHAPTER 5

WORKSHEET 5.1: THE SALT WITHIN

PART 1: LEARNING TO RECOGNIZE

Reflection Prompts

Think of the quiet contributors in your life—at home, at work or in the community. Who keeps things going but is rarely acknowledged? Who in your family or workplace plays the role of 'salt'—always present, always giving, but seldom appreciated? When was the last time you thanked them genuinely?

Action Step

Write down the names of three 'salt-like' people in your life and one way you can express your appreciation to each of them today, not later.

✍ _____

_____

_____

PART 2: LEARNING TO EXPRESS

Sometimes we support and show up for everyone—yet feel unseen or unheard. Use this space to notice where you've been quiet, not because you lack ideas, but because you've learned to stay in the background.

Reflection Prompts

- Do I often take pride in being dependable but secretly feel unseen?
- Do I hold back my ideas out of fear of judgement?
- Do I confuse humility with silence?

Action Steps

Think of one situation this week where you will aim to express yourself properly—it could be an idea or drawing a boundary or making a request.

✍ _____
_____
_____

Remind yourself: Salt doesn't stop being salt if it shines—it only makes the dish more vibrant.

✍ _____
_____
_____

Part 3: Balancing Recognition and Expression

True balance is when contribution is recognized by others and expression is encouraged by one's own self.

Reflection Prompts

- How can I create a culture—at home or at work—where quiet contributors are noticed?
- If I am salt, what gentle step can I take to ensure I don't dissolve without a trace?

Key Insight

Salt may be invisible, but it is never absent. When recognition and expression meet, every dish—and every relationship—becomes richer.

∼

CHAPTER 6

Worksheet 6.1: Breaking the Loop: The A-R-I-S-E Model

To rise above painful patterns, we need more than external change—we need an inner shift. The acronym A-R-I-S-E offers a step-by-step compass that you can use in your own life.

A – Awareness: The first step is simply to notice the pattern.

- What keeps repeating in your life?
- Do you often feel dismissed, not chosen, or undervalued?
- Which situations or relationships leave you feeling like this has happened before?

Awareness shines the light on cycles we otherwise stumble through in the dark.

Exercise: Write down one pattern in your relationships, work, or personal life that you've noticed repeating.

✍ _____

_____

_____

R – Release and Heal: Awareness is powerful, but unless we release old emotions, they keep recycling. Healing means allowing yourself to feel regret, anger, or grief—and then letting it go. It's not about forgetting the past, but about not letting it control you any longer.

Exercise: List one old emotion that you are still carrying. Next to it, write a small ritual or practice you could use to release it (like journaling, meditation, forgiveness, talking it out, etc.).

✍ _____

_____

_____

I – INSTALL NEW SCRIPTS: Old inner scripts like 'I am not enough' or 'This is all I deserve' must be replaced. Rewiring means deliberately creating new affirmations and beliefs:

- 'I am worthy of love and respect.'
- 'I am capable.'

Each time the old story rises, install a new one.

Exercise: Write down one limiting belief you often catch yourself repeating. Then write the empowering belief you'd like to replace it with.

✍ _____

_____

_____

S – SET BOUNDARIES: Healing doesn't mean tolerating what hurts you. Boundaries are a form of self-respect. They are not walls to shut people out but gates that let in only what nourishes you.

Exercise: Identify one place in your life where you need a clearer boundary (with a person, a habit, or a situation). Write the first step you could take to set it.

✍ _____

_____

_____

E – Energy Shift: Finally, shift your energy. Healing changes how you see yourself, and that, in turn, changes what you attract. Surround yourself with healthier influences—people, practices and environments that uplift you.

Exercise: Write down two ways you could shift your energy this week (like spending time with positive people, decluttering your space or adding a daily gratitude practice).

👍 _____

_____

_____

REFLECTION PROMPT

We don't move on by forgetting; we move on by remembering differently—without rehearsing the hurt.

How does this line apply to your own journey right now?

👍 _____

_____

_____

CHAPTER 7

WORKSHEET 7.1: BUILDING TRUST THROUGH BETTER COMMUNICATION

Assumptions, even with good intentions, but without the right approach, can damage trust. Clear, open communication is the key. Use this worksheet to reflect, practise and strengthen your communication habits.

Part 1: Pause before You Pounce

Recall a recent situation where you jumped to a conclusion. What happened? What assumption did you make? How did it affect your relationship with the other person?

Example: Your colleague didn't reply to your email for two days. You assumed they were ignoring you, so you sent a curt message. Later, you found out that they had been unwell.

 _____

_____

Part 2: Replace 'Why Did You?' with 'Can You Help Me Understand?'

Reframe questions you often ask in a defensive way into open-ended ones.

Example: Instead of asking 'Why did you come home so late?', try saying 'Can you help me understand what kept you back today?' This shifts the tone from accusation to curiosity.

 _____

_____

Part 3: Facts First, Feelings Second

Think of a time you confused what you saw with what you felt. Separate them into what is fact and what is your interpretation. Then see how you can communicate your question better.

Example:

Fact: 'I saw you speaking with someone at the cafe yesterday.'
Interpretation: 'You must be hiding something from me.'

Better Communication: 'I noticed you were with someone yesterday—could you tell me about it?'

 _____

_____

Part 4: Assume Good Intent, until Proven Otherwise

List three people you trust. Write how assuming good intent could help you deal with any conflict.

Example: Your friend cancelled lunch at the last minute. You assumed they didn't value your time. Later, you learned they had a family emergency. If you had assumed good intent first, you would have saved yourself the hurt.

 _____

_____

Part 5: Express before It Festers

Write about one thing you've been holding yourself back from expressing. How can you say it respectfully?

Example: Instead of staying silent and building resentment, try saying: 'I feel overwhelmed when I'm the only one handling household chores. Can we divide them more evenly?' This prevents the issue from growing into a bigger conflict.

_____

_____

Key Insight

Trust is not built by avoiding problems, but by communicating through them. Pause, clarify and share openly—it's harder in the moment, but it makes relationships stronger in the long run.

∽

Worksheet 7.2: Beyond Right and Wrong—Living with Empathy

Life is rarely black and white. Often, choices are made under pressure, fear or helplessness. These choices may cause pain—sometimes unintentionally. This worksheet is designed to help you pause, reflect and approach situations with more empathy and less judgement.

Part 1: Reflect on a Painful Memory

Think of a time when someone's actions hurt you deeply.
- What happened?
- What assumption did you make about their intention?
- Looking back, could there have been another layer to their actions, a reason you did not know at the time?

✍ _____

_____

_____

Part 2: Recognize Grey Areas

List two situations in your life where the choices made (by you or someone else) were not clearly right or wrong, but were moulded by the circumstances.

✍ _____

_____

_____

How did those choices affect you or the others?

✍ _____

_____

_____

Part 3: Pause before Judging

The next time you feel wronged, ask yourself:
- Could there be something I don't know yet?
- What pain or pressure could the other person have been under?

Reflection Prompt: Before reacting, remind yourself:

'I don't know the whole story yet. What I see may only be a part of it.'

Part 4: Empathy in Action

Think of someone in your life right now with whom you feel tension.

Write one empathetic question you could ask them instead of holding assumptions.

Example: 'Can you help me understand what you were going through when that happened?'

 _____

_____

Part 5: The Practice of Forgiveness

Forgiveness does not erase the pain, but it can ease the burden.
- Name one person you might try to forgive, even a little, for your own peace of mind?
- What would be a first step towards that forgiveness (a conversation, a letter, a change in perspective)?

 _____

_____

Part 6: Self-Compassion

Sometimes the hardest person to forgive is one's own self.

- Write down one mistake you keep judging yourself for.
- Now, reframe it: 'I made this choice because at that time I was ____ (afraid/helpless/confused/trying my best). I am learning from it now.'

✍ _____
_____

Key Insight

Life is complicated, layered and nuanced. The goal is not to justify hurtful actions, but to approach them with understanding. A little empathy and a little forgiveness—for others and for ourselves—make life gentler, lighter and more liveable.

CHAPTER 8

Worksheet 8.1: Navigating Life's Crossroads

Life's hardest choices are rarely about right vs wrong. They are often about two rights that cannot coexist. This worksheet will help you reflect on your own crossroads with honesty, empathy and courage.

Identifying Your Crossroad

Write down a situation where you had (or still have) to choose between two equally important paths.

Example: I was offered a promotion at work that required me to move to another city.

- *Option A: Take the promotion.*
  What it represents: Career growth and financial stability.

- *Option B: Stay in my city.*
  What it represents: Being present for ageing parents and closeness to family.

✍ _____
_____
_____

Naming the Cost

Every choice carries a price. Write down what you would gain and what you would lose with each option.

- **Option A (Relocate):**
  Gain: Higher income, new opportunities, prestige.
  Loss: Time with parents, being there for family.

- **Option B (Stay):**
  Gain: Closeness with family, peace of mind about parents' health.
  Loss: Career advancement, higher salary.

✍ _____
_____
_____

Your Conscience Test

Ask yourself: 'Which choice will allow me to sleep peacefully at night? Which choice will my conscience accept?'

Example: I realized that if something happened to my parents while I was away, I would never forgive myself. My conscience told me that family came first for me at this stage of life.

✍ _____
_____
_____

∼

Worksheet 8.2: Honouring Empty Spaces

We all carry 'empty spaces'—absences, longings, unfulfilled dreams. This worksheet will help you reflect on those spaces with empathy, patience and honesty.

Naming Your Empty Space

What is that one area of your life where you feel something is missing? (a parent's love, a friendship lost, a dream unfulfilled)

Example: I never had a close relationship with my father.

 _____

_____

The Longing beneath It

What do you truly long for in this space? (love, security, recognition, companionship, affirmation, guidance)

Example: What I really longed for was guidance—someone to teach me how to navigate life with confidence.

 _____

_____

The Impact on You

How has this empty space shaped you? Has it made you more independent? More sensitive? More guarded? More creative?

Example: Because I didn't have that guidance, I became resourceful. I also developed more empathy for others who struggle quietly.

 _____

_____

Honouring the Space

Instead of rushing to 'fill' it, how can you honour this empty space? (journaling, art, conversations, prayer, self-care, service)

Example: I can honour it by expressing my feelings through writing and by being the mentor I wish I had for someone younger.

 _____

_____

PATIENCE WITH THE UNKNOWN

What would patience look like here? (accepting the ache without bitterness, trusting that healing or connection may come in its own time)

Example: Patience means not blaming myself or others, but allowing relationships to evolve naturally if they are meant to.

 _____

_____

TURNING THE SPACE INTO STRENGTH

How can this space empower you instead of weaken you?

Example: My longing for guidance has made me passionate about helping others find their way. What I lacked has become my motivation to give.

 _____

_____

KEY INSIGHT

Empty spaces are not flaws. They are invitations—to grow gentler, deeper and more patient. You may one day see them filled in unexpected ways, or they may remain—but they'll become the still corners of the heart where warmth quietly settles.

∼

CHAPTER 9

Worksheet 9.1: The Stains We Carry

Naming the Stain

What memory or experience keeps resurfacing, even when you think it's behind you? It could be a loss, a hurtful word, a moment of kindness or a turning point.

Example: I still remember the time I was excluded from a group I wanted to belong to.

_____

How It Returns

When does this memory resurface? Perhaps there is a smell, a song, a place or a person that brings it back?

Example: It comes up whenever I hear laughter from a group I'm not a part of.

_____

The Impact

How does this 'stain' affect you when it reappears? Does it make you withdraw, smile, ache, avoid or learn something about yourself?

Example: I feel insecure and left out, even if the situation today is different.

_____

Sweet Stains vs Sore Stains

Which memories feel like sweet stains—reminders that warm your heart? Which ones feel like sore stains—reminders you'd rather avoid?

Example: A teacher's kind words stay with me as encouragement (sweet stain). The memory of a fight with my sibling years ago still hurts (sore stain).

 _____

_____

Integrating the Stain

If you could let this memory instruct you instead of imprison you, what lesson could it teach?

Example: Being excluded taught me the value of including others.

 _____

_____

A Small Ritual of Release

What simple ritual could you do to acknowledge this memory and carry it differently?

Example: I will write the memory down, thank it for the lesson it taught me and then fold the paper into my journal as a reminder that I own the story now.

 _____

_____

Key Insight

Just as turmeric is antiseptic even while it stains, our past can both wound and heal. The goal is not to erase the marks, but to let them soften us, deepen us and guide us.

∽

CHAPTER 10

WORKSHEET 10.1: THINKING, DOING AND DECIDING WISELY

SUGRIVA'S TRAP: WHEN WE ONLY THINK

Endless Reflection without Movement = Stagnation

Reflection Prompts

What am I currently overthinking instead of acting on?

✍ _____

What fear hides behind my hesitation?

✍ _____

What is that one small step that I could take today—even imperfectly?

✍ _____

Has there been a situation in my life where I 'saw' but didn't 'act'?

✍ _____

Takeaway: Thought without action is wasted potential.

RAVANA'S MISTAKE: WHEN WE ONLY DO

Action without Reflection = Destruction

Reflection Prompts

What decision or reaction have I rushed into recently?

✍ _____

What was I trying to avoid by acting so fast? Was it discomfort, silence or the act of waiting?

✍ _____

What could I have done differently if I had paused to think?

✍ _____

Your Thought Journal

Takeaway: Haste may feel like relief, but wisdom comes from pause.

Hanuman's Way: When Thought and Action Meet

Balanced Reflection + Courageous Action = Wisdom in Motion

Reflection Prompts

One recent choice where I balanced reflection and action:

✍ _____

What helped me find that balance? Was it faith, clarity, stillness, or the presence of a mentor perhaps?

✍ _____

What is that one area of life right now where I can apply this balance?

✍ _____

Takeaway: The beauty lies not in doing more, but in doing mindfully.

Turning Lessons into Practice

Think—Act—Learn—Repeat

My pattern is more:

☐ Overthinking ☐ Overdoing ☐ Balance

If Overthinking:

- Set a 48-hour action rule—decide and act within two days.

If Overdoing:

- Adopt a reflection ritual—pause 10 minutes before saying yes/no.

THE EXPERIENCE SECRET

Right decisions come from experience. Experience comes from wrong decisions.

Reflection Prompts

What 'wrong' decision from my past has been my best teacher?

✍ _____

What did I learn from it that no success could have taught me?

✍ _____

Takeaway: Don't fear wrong turns—fear standing still.

THIS WEEK'S PRACTICE PLAN

Transform insight into movement. Pick one area to work on this week, decide your action and commit to when you'll do it by.

Reflection Goal	Action Step	Timeframe
_____	_____	_____
_____	_____	_____
_____	_____	_____

REFLECTION AFFIRMATION

'I will not fear wrong decisions more than I fear indecision. I will think sincerely, act courageously and learn humbly.'

∼

WORKSHEET 10.2: THE CAKE OF CONNECTION—BUILDING RELATIONSHIPS THAT NOURISH AND LAST

THE REAL MEANING OF RELATIONSHIPS

A relationship isn't a destination—it's an ongoing journey.

It's not defined by a single celebration or milestone but by the everyday moments that follow—the laughter, the listening, the forgiveness and the choice to stay kind.

Reflection Prompts

What makes my closest relationships feel truly meaningful?

 _____
_____

How do I make my presence felt and show that I care when there's no special occasion?

_____
_____

THE FOUNDATION—THE CAKE ITSELF

The cake is the core—built with trust, honesty, respect, empathy and consistency. Without this foundation, even the sweetest gestures eventually crumble.

Reflection Prompts

Which 'ingredients' are strong in my relationships?

 _____
_____

What do I need to pay more attention to—trust, honesty, boundaries or patience?

 _____
_____

THE ICING—WARMTH AND EXPRESSION

The icing is how we show affection—through words, gestures, humour, time and thoughtfulness. It makes relationships sweeter, but only when the base beneath it is firm.

Reflection Prompts

How do I express affection or appreciation meaningfully?

✍ _____

_____

When do I rely too much on superficial gestures instead of emotional presence?

✍ _____

_____

The Cherry—The Extras

The cherry is everything external—gifts, travel, events, photos, social media posts, public praise. They're lovely, but they can't save a weak bond.

Reflection Prompts

What 'cherries' do I tend to overvalue in my relationships?

✍ _____

_____

How can I enjoy these extras without losing sight of the real connection beneath?

✍ _____

_____

The Oven—Time and Patience

A good cake takes time to bake. Rush it, and it burns on the outside while staying raw inside. Relationships, too, need space, patience and rhythm—to grow naturally, not forcefully.

Reflection Prompts

Where am I rushing growth in a relationship instead of allowing it to mature?

✍ _____

_____

How can I practise more patience—with others, or with myself?

✍ _____

_____

The Recipe for Strong Connections

Ingredient	Description	My Score (1–10)
Trust	The quiet confidence that we have each other's backs.	
Communication	Speaking honestly, listening fully.	
Respect	Valuing differences as much as similarities.	
Patience	Giving time to understand and heal.	
Empathy	Seeing through another's eyes before reacting.	
Humour	Laughing together and trying to lighten the load.	

The Life Lesson

No amount of decoration can save a cake that's raw inside. Similarly, no amount of gestures or gifts can save a relationship that isn't real inside.

Action Steps

What's one thing that I can do this week to strengthen a key relationship in my life?

✍ _____

_____

What's one habit I can release that adds decoration, not depth?

✍ _____

_____

CHAPTER 11

Worksheet 11.1: The Myth of 'Having It All'

Thought Starter

We often chase the idea of a perfect life. But life is like a home-cooked meal, with one dish too spicy, and one a little bland. And yet, when cooked with love, even that imperfect meal can warm the heart.

Reflection Questions

Define Your 'All'

What does 'having it all' mean for you right now—not society's version, not social media's version, but *yours*?

- ☐ Security
- ☐ Growth
- ☐ Love
- ☐ Purpose
- ☐ Balance
- ☐ Peace
- ☐ Other: _____

Perfection vs Wholeness

Write down one are where you're chasing perfection.

✍ _____

_____

Now write what 'wholeness' might look like instead.

✍ _____
_____

The Ladder and the Snake

Life doesn't always go as planned. When was the last time you faced a setback (a snake) that later led to growth (a ladder)?

✍ _____
_____

Your Recipe for a Full Life

If life were your thali, what five 'dishes' would you want to fill it with—not perfectly, but meaningfully?

✍ _____
_____

KEY INSIGHTS

- 'Having it all' is not about getting everything; it's about appreciating what's already on your plate.
- Control, perfection and guarantees are illusions.
- Growth, love, peace and connection—these are the real 'all'.
- Imperfection doesn't make life less beautiful, it makes it *real*.

REFLECTION PROMPT

What can you appreciate, even if it isn't perfect?

✍ _____
_____

Notes

Scan this QR code to access the detailed notes.

About the Author

Gaur Gopal Das studied electrical engineering at the College of Engineering, Pune. After a brief stint with Hewlett-Packard, he chose to dedicate his life to spirituality and service, joining an ashram in downtown Mumbai.

For more than two decades, Gaur Gopal Das has travelled the globe, addressing corporate leaders, universities and charitable organizations, and has spoken at the United Nations in New York. His global reach grew exponentially in 2016 when he took his message online. Today, with over 2.5 billion views on his videos and a following of more than 25 million across social media platforms, he continues to inspire millions to find purpose, balance and happiness.

Gaur Gopal Das is the author of two national bestsellers and has been conferred with several honours, including the prestigious Global Changemaker of the Year Award at the Dadasaheb Phalke International Film Festival in 2020 and an honorary doctorate (DLitt) from Kalinga Institute of Industrial Technology (KIIT), Bhubaneswar. Recognized as one of the most influential monks in the world today, Gaur Gopal Das leads a movement dedicated to helping people live more meaningful and fulfilled lives.

HarperCollins *Publishers* India

At HarperCollins India, we believe in telling the best stories and finding the widest readership for our books in every format possible. We started publishing in 1992; a great deal has changed since then, but what has remained constant is the passion with which our authors write their books, the love with which readers receive them, and the sheer joy and excitement that we as publishers feel in being a part of the publishing process.

Over the years, we've had the pleasure of publishing some of the finest writing from the subcontinent and around the world, including several award-winning titles and some of the biggest bestsellers in India's publishing history. But nothing has meant more to us than the fact that millions of people have read the books we published, and that somewhere, a book of ours might have made a difference.

As we look to the future, we go back to that one word—a word which has been a driving force for us all these years.

Read.